Shirley Bowers
From History to H

Shirley Bowers

From History to Hope

A Journey of Healing and Reconciliation

Verlag Gottfried Bernard
Solingen

© 2006 Verlag Gottfried Bernard
  2013 revised Edition

Verlag Gottfried Bernard
Heidstraße 2a
42719 Solingen
E-Mail: verlag.gottfriedbernard@t-online.de
Internet: www.gbernard.de

ISBN 978-3-938677-16-2
Order No. 175616

Cover Design by Stefanie Riewe and Daniel Bernard
Image source:
Beautiful background – sunset sky, bright sun shines through clouds
Copyright Igor Zh., 2013
Ancient map of the world Copyright javarman, 2013
Used under license from Shutterstock.com

Typeset by Satz & Medien Wieser, Stolberg, Germany

Printed in Germany

Contents

Acknowledgements

It is difficult to know where to begin as so many people have influenced me over the years and without each one I would never have begun to fulfil this task. However, let me first start with my own family, because without the love and support of my husband Tony and children David, Alison, Kevin and Jonathan, I would never have had the courage to face my pain and allow God to heal me. Tony in particular has in many ways paid the price for my calling, for the times when I am away and the hours spent writing this book. I also know that he has and will continue to receive many blessings from God. Thank you darling, I really do appreciate you!

Secondly to Vanessa Murphy who together with me has spent many hours poring over letters, as well as this manuscript, using her skill as an editor. Thank you, Vanessa. I know that without your love, support and prayers this wouldn't have been possible. I also know that God has and will continue to bless you abundantly for all your dedication and hard work.

To the team who accompanied me around Ireland; Annette Quail, Katie Sims, Vanessa Murphy, Beryl and Lance Ayres, Phyllis Forsythe as well as Rev Edward Wright and Rev Stephen Talbot who came for the first part of the trip and Derek Murphy who came with us in 2003. Thank you for sharing this time with me and the many laughs as well as the tears. I appreciate each one of you.

To the core team and intercessors who have supported me in prayer. My love and sincere thanks go to each one of you. You know what you all mean to me.

To Pastor Peter Morris, who for a number of years was our Pastor, but due to ill health had to step down. Thank you Peter for all your love and continual support. To Rev Scott Watts, who heard God's call and has taken his place. Many Blessings Scott.

To the many friends we have made along the way in England, Ireland and Uganda, many of whom are mentioned in the book.

To two dear friends and brothers in Christ, Rev Stephen Talbot for his continual support and encouragement, and Pastor John Mulinde, whose obedience to bring God's word to England, began this journey.

To my dear friends Annette, Vanessa and Katie, three very dedicated prayer partners. I, like Paul, in Philippians 1v 4-5 would like to thank them for their partnership in the Gospel. I don't know what I would have done without you! God knew what He was doing when He brought each one of you into my life and I thank Him daily for you.

To my son Jonathan. Thank you for your continual support and for leading us in worship and into God's presence.

I want to end these acknowledgements by mentioning a special couple, Rev Robin and Margaret Mann. For without their obedience, this journey would never have been possible. They came into my life at a God-given time and through Robin's teaching and their love, I received amazing healing and began to know God as my loving Father. Robin and Margaret, this comes with my love and sincere thanks for all you have done for me and for God's Kingdom.

However, I know that each person above and those mentioned in the book would agree with me, that there is only one to whom this should be dedicated and that's to the glory of God!

Foreword

In 1996, having received a prophetic word from the Lord concerning Europe, I set out in obedience to go and proclaim it, starting in England. I thought this was going to be a one-off mission, but I was grossly mistaken. In all my wildest expectations, I never dreamed the fruit that has come out of that mission, one of which is this wonderful book.

The very first church that opened its doors to me was in a small village called Hemingford Grey, in Huntingdonshire, England. I shared the word with all the zeal I could marshal. Although the response was not overwhelming, there was enough there for the vicar of the church and three other members of the congregation to accept an invitation to visit Uganda during our annual revival camp meeting.

In that particular camp, in January 1997, we were dealing with the corporate sins of Uganda, majoring mainly on the issues of bloodshed, unresolved injustice, and spirit of vengeance that prevailed at that time. Many ethnic, social and faith-based groups came forward and engaged in identification repentance that drew wailing and many tears all day long for the entire week. Such corporate brokenness had never before been seen in our nation.

Whatever took place in that camp meeting somehow ministered to our British visitors in a deep way that spoke to their hearts about their own nation. It revealed to them facts about their national history that needed to be addressed, in order to bring healing to the wounds that history had brought upon the United Kingdom.

The team (Rev Stephen Talbot, one gentleman and two ladies) carried this burden back to England and began to work on the healing of the land by addressing these issues. One of the ladies was Shirley Bowers. Later, I came to know Shirley better and she became one of my prayer partners. Little did I realise that the seed sown in those meetings was going to have so much bearing on her future, and even bring out her destiny, as has happened.

Shirley stood firmly by her vicar Stephen as he tried his best to bring the churches in Huntingdon into unity, prayer networking and reviewing the history of their town in relationship to the land of England and Ireland. Soon unity and prayer networks began to develop in the area, and so did their revelation of the significance of their local area in the history of the whole of the United Kingdom.

It was at that time they discovered the significance of Huntingdon being the birthplace of Oliver Cromwell, who had played such a key role in shaping the history of the UK and its politics. They also discovered the causes he stood for, as well as the injustices involved as he pursued his dream. This opened a Pandora's box that kept expanding.

There came a moment when I sincerely doubted if the team would have the faith and will to pursue this matter to a conclusive end in the spirit. Later, my fears were quelled when I discovered that Shirley had risen up, contrary to all her natural character traits, and taken leadership of this noble cause. She and her team gave themselves to research, to interpret and to pay any cost involved to address the negative impact of what history had brought between the English and the Irish through the Cromwell era. They prayed in faith that God would begin to reverse this cycle and heal the land. As the team developed into a formal ministry, they made several trips to Northern Ireland and the Irish republic, meeting with civic and spiritual leaders to work for reconciliation and healing.

I witness in amazement how the Lord has led Shirley's team step by step, and also given them favour to succeed in each of these endeavours. Without doubt, what Shirley has got to share in this book is not just theory, but the fruit of holding and walking faithfully in the revelation that the Lord was progressively releasing. The great lessons she shares could contribute to solving the problems in Europe and the deep underlying spiritual issues. I want to recommend this book as a handbook to all who have a burden for Europe. What you are about to read may change you so much that you will end up becoming an agent of change in your society. Please read this book prayerfully and may the High One give you the grace to rise above the ashes of yesterday so as to build for tomorrow.

With many regards and respect for Shirley Bowers and her team, John Mulinde.

Foreword to the Second Edition

The first edition of *From History to Hope* was published in 2006. Now seven years later, you will be able to read the story in the light of all that has happened in the England/Ireland situation during the intervening years. There has been an extraordinary softening of attitudes, particularly among former hard-line politicians. There has been a marked decrease in violence and a growing sense of peace and normality. And not least the historic visit of Her Majesty the Queen to the Republic of Ireland. Clearly there has been a decisive shift in the spiritual landscape over the past few years and who could doubt the part Arise Ministries, guided by the Holy Spirit, has played in that?

So read the book, be inspired, give thanks for all that God has done and pray that He will bring to completion all that He has begun in your own life, in that of the Arise team and the people of Ireland.

I was privileged to play a small part in the beginning of this story and I pray that the second edition of this book will bless all who read it and that its outworking will bear much fruit for the Kingdom of God.

Rev Robin Mann.

Introduction

When I was in the process of writing this book, someone said to me "What makes you think anyone would be interested in reading about you?" Once upon a time that statement would have devastated me, and I would have given up there and then. However the difference now is that I know who I am. I am an ordinary woman with an extraordinary God.

If anyone had said to me when I was younger that one day I would write a book, I would have laughed! I never would have thought in my wildest dreams that this was possible, as anyone who knew me then would tell you. However, when God steps in things change, and that is what this story is all about. How God changed my life around from rejection to acceptance, from fear to faith, from failure to victory. This is God's story. My prayer is that as you read this, you will hear Him speak to you, and as His Word says "*Call to me and I will answer you and tell you great and unsearchable things you do not know.*" (Jeremiah 33 v 3).

I pray too that this will be a tool for you to use to help you unravel some of the things you have struggled with for so long. For you to be able to see that God longs to bring light into your darkness and hope where there has been despair. I pray that your faith will rise and give birth to new prayer for your family, your church, your town and your country. To realise that you and they don't have to keep repeating the same old mistakes. God is a God who longs to renew your mind; "*Therefore I urge you brothers, in view of God's mercy, to offer your bodies as a living sacrifices, holy and pleasing to God. This is your spiritual act of worship. Do not conform any longer to the pattern of this world, but be transformed by the renewing of your mind, then you will be able to test and approve what God's will is, his good pleasing and perfect will.*" (Romans 12 v 1-2). I pray it will encourage you to believe that God has a plan for you and that He will guide you if you seek His will and purpose. If your heart is to go where God leads, then be prepared for surprises!

I also pray that it will inspire you to look again at your history to see if there is anything that has blocked God fulfilling His purpose for you, your family or nation. Where has the enemy distracted and distorted the truth? What patterns are still being repeated?

My prayer is that when you have finished this book, it will only be the beginning for you. The beginning of a life surrendered to God; The beginning of knowing that you are God's beloved child; The beginning of a renewed faith and prayer life; The beginning of you knowing your part in setting people free.

My love and prayers go with you as you turn each page.

Many blessings
Shirley

Chapter One
In the Beginning

The Date: 11th September 2002.
The Place: Drogheda, Republic of Ireland.
The Occasion: Retracing Cromwell's Steps.

Who would have believed this? Me, Shirley Bowers, leading a team of Christians of mixed denominations to say we are sorry for what Oliver Cromwell had done and the pain he had caused all those years ago. For it was on this day in 1649 that Cromwell and his men took the town of Drogheda. As I think back on all that has happened to make this possible, I marvel at the awesomeness of God. Only He could have done this. *"No, not by might nor even power but by my spirit says the Lord."* (Zechariah 4 v 6). Only you, oh God, could have worked this miracle in my life.

When did it all begin? Well it was back in September 1986, when a new minister, Rev Robin Mann, came to our Methodist Church in Huntingdon. I was going through a difficult time. I was recovering from the death of a very close friend when I received a telephone call telling me that my grandfather had collapsed in the street and had been taken to hospital. Our second son Kevin had been in and out of hospital since he was a baby and our teenage daughter Alison had recently suffered a nasty accident, which involved her having many operations before eventually having her kneecaps removed. As a result of this, I was feeling really low. So I asked if I could see Robin and his wife Margaret.

I was so nervous that day that I began to wonder if I had made a mistake. What if it all sounds silly and they think I am just making a fuss? There are lots of people much worse off than me. However, as soon as I met them, I felt totally at ease. It was as if I had known them all my life. For someone as shy as I was, that was a miracle! As I poured out my heart to them, I can remember saying that I could analyse myself completely, but couldn't do anything about it. Robin and Margaret, who are now very dear friends, listened patiently. I had never felt I could share like this with anyone before, but they showed me nothing but love and concern. Before they left, they asked if they could pray with me. Although ministers and friends had prayed before, I was soon to realise that this time it was to be different. They stood and very gently laid hands on me. I had never experienced this sort of prayer, I felt a total peace.

Robin told me that he knew of an organisation called *Wholeness Through Christ* (WTC) and he believed they could help me. He shared a little of what WTC was about and it sounded very interesting. So, a few days later, he came to see Tony, my husband, and I about going away on an "Introduction to Wholeness" weekend. He said that if we felt this was something we wanted to do, he would arrange everything and they even offered to have our children while we were away. Tony and I had never done anything like this before, in fact we had never left the children. However, we thought this could be a good opportunity for us to spend time together, so we accepted their kind offer.

The course was held in Derbyshire, a beautiful part of the United Kingdom and one I had never been to before. I was overcome with excitement from the moment we left home and I was not to be disappointed. I knew from the beginning I was in the right place because, for the first time in my life, I heard how God longs to touch those areas of our lives that have been damaged by past experiences and how they can create a barrier between us and Him.

The Wholeness Through Christ teaching is based around Psalm 103 v 3-5: "*Praise the Lord, who forgives all your sins and heals all your diseases, who redeems your life from the pit and crowns you with love and compassion, who satisfies your desires with good things so that your youth is renewed like the eagle's.*" He heals all our diseases. We know we are ransomed, healed, restored and forgiven; this is the truth, won for us on the cross. However, when we become Christians, we do not automatically become perfect, that is the ongoing work of the Holy Spirit in our lives, as He reveals to us those broken areas that need His touch. For example, we can sometimes be so hurt, that we put up barriers to protect ourselves. This makes life more bearable at the time, but it also shuts out God's love and can leave a root of bitterness or unforgiveness, which can cause us to react in ways that are wrong.

I spent a great deal of time that weekend in tears, but as usual, I hid it from others so that no one would know. However, God knew. After one of the sessions, a lady who had been sitting in front of me turned round. She told me that during the morning she had been given a picture for me. It was of a beautiful rose. She felt that God was saying, "All I am doing is taking away the broken petals." I didn't know it then, but this picture was to play an important part in my story.

On the Saturday afternoon, Tony and I sat talking in the lounge area. I remember looking up and seeing a lady walking towards us. Being so shy, I really hoped that she was heading for someone else, but she wasn't. "Hello" she said as she sat down. "I hope you don't mind, but I had to come and speak to you. Earlier today, I was given a picture of a queen on horseback dressed in fine clothes. It was you!" My stomach did a turn, I would never have thought of myself that way. She continued "God wants you to know that it is like Esther 4 v 14." I had no idea what this meant as it wasn't a passage I was familiar with. I thanked her and later I looked up the scripture; "*For if you remain silent at this time, relief and deliverance for the Jews will arise from another place, but you and your family will perish. And who knows but that you have come to royal position for such a time as this.*" What could this mean? I really had no idea.

That weekend was to be a turning point in my life. The teaching I heard and the gentle way in which it was put, helped me to begin to see that things I had thought about myself for years could be changed. There was an excitement beginning to rise in me. I don't think I had any understanding why, but I knew this was going to make a difference, not only to me as a person but also to my Christian walk.

So my journey began. God had a lot to do in my life. I certainly did not feel like a beautiful rose or a queen. I was the third child, conceived at a time when my parents already had two very young children. The war had only been ended a year and money was tight. They had not planned on me coming along and I was often told that I was a mistake. The message I got, rightly or wrongly, was "I shouldn't really have been born. They would all be better off if I wasn't here." My father had always told me that I was the ugliest baby ever born. I didn't give this much thought at the time, but as I grew up, I realised that I had a very low opinion of myself, and if anyone paid me a compliment, I would be so embarrassed. I hadn't realised that words could affect me so much. I am sure that my father didn't mean it the way I took it, but it did affect me badly. I felt rejected and insignificant and became shy and lacking in confidence. It became easier for me to put myself down before anyone else did. It was less painful that way. I was shown that God loved me before I was even born and that I am precious in His sight just the way I am. I knew that Jesus died so that I could be forgiven, so I in turn needed to forgive my father and this allowed the healing love of Jesus to flow into me. I was able to see that my parents had not meant to hurt me. By forgiving the words said and asking God to forgive me for my wrong attitudes, I began to accept myself and receive the love of God that I had never really known.

While I was on a WTC course in 1988, an intercessor sent a message to the team for me. She said that as she was praying, she had a picture/vision. It was of me being lifted off a boat with a net and God said "This isn't right, you're going to travel first class". I remember thinking what a silly picture. What on earth can it mean? Surely if you were going to travel first class, you wouldn't be lifted off with a net. Besides I didn't even travel much. At the end of the prayer time, we were encouraged to write down any pictures or scriptures that had been given to help us remember what God done. So I added this picture to my paper and I didn't think about it again until much later. I had no idea what God was planning.

In 1990, Robin, our minister held a teaching day at church. I was thrilled as I wanted to learn more about the Bible and thought this would be a perfect opportunity. We were given three Bible passages and we had to choose which one we wanted to look at and meditate on. I started to panic, which passage was the best? I didn't know what to do, I was so confused. Once I had picked one, I was then worried that I had picked the wrong one. I tried so hard to concentrate, but I just couldn't. Frustration set in and tears started to flow. I just didn't know what to do. Later on, when people started to share what they had got out of their passage, it made me feel even worse as all my time had been spent trying to work out which passage I should look at.

I thank God for Robin. He has such a sensitive and gentle spirit, I never felt pressured in any way, and that day wasn't any different. He came to me and gently put his hand on my arm and asked if I wanted to talk. At that moment, I had no idea what the problem was, so initially I declined. However, God had used him and his wife Margaret in my healing process many times and I could see that dealing with this pain would be my next stage.

So, on April 10th 1990, I arrived on their doorstep. I still didn't know what was causing the problem. I thought I was just being over-sensitive and that they would think I was making a fuss about nothing. It was just me getting it wrong again and I would look a fool in front of them both. I needn't have worried though, for God was in control. Robin, as usual, had been praying beforehand for the ministry time. He said he had been given two pieces of scripture for me, one was Deuteronomy 28 v 1-14, the blessings of obedience and the other was Joshua 1 v 1-9. As Joshua was one of the passages that we had been given on the study day, I wondered what God was trying to say to me. My fears were soon laid to rest and it wasn't long before a story from my school days came to mind.

When I was at junior school, we were doing a maths test. One of the questions was "If you go to bed at 7 and get up at 7, how many hours have you been in bed?" I remember thinking that I hadn't a clue, so I guessed "12". When it came to marking the papers, to my amazement I was the only one in the class to get this question right. At which point, the teacher called me out in front of the class and asked "How did you know this answer?" I didn't know what to say. I hated everyone looking at me and even now I can remember how I felt. Somehow, I plucked up enough courage to tell her that it was a guess. The look on her face told me she didn't believe me. She turned to the whole class and told them that I was lying and that I had cheated. I was far too frightened to say anything. She told me to hold out my hands and then proceeded to punish me severely by hitting me hard with a ruler. This left me very confused. If I am punished for getting it right, what will happen if I get it wrong? Fear took over and from then on I hated school. I was so frightened that I spent most of my time worrying in case I got it wrong, and I became an easy target for bullying.

As I shared the story, I felt like that little girl all over again. Fear just filled my body. I was so frightened I was going to get it wrong. I began to sob and sob. Robin and Margaret just came alongside me and their gentle touch was so reassuring, I knew I could forgive my teacher for what she had done. As I did this, the healing love of Jesus flooded in, and where the love of Jesus is, fear has to go, and He set me free.

At the end of any prayer time, Robin and Margaret prayed for the Holy Spirit to come and fill up the empty places. On this occasion, the prayer was that love and peace would replace the fear and confusion. During the prayer time, I felt as if someone had put a very heavy weight in my left hand. I told Robin, but he said nothing. It got heavier and heavier. I told him again and still he said nothing. Suddenly I became aware of what it was. It was a short dagger. What could it mean? All sorts of thoughts went through my mind. However, before I had a chance to say anything, Robin started to speak. He said:

"The Lord calls you into leadership of His people in the spiritual battle against evil. For too long, the people of God have been in the wilderness. The time is now approaching for them to enter into their true inheritance. As God called and commissioned Joshua, so now He calls and commissions you. The words of scripture in Joshua 1 v 1-9 are therefore God's word for you today. As a modern Joan of Arc, you are to lead the people of God over the Jordan and into the land of His promise. The Jordan of today will be for you a significant crossing point of no return.

You are fully equipped for this task. You already have everything that is necessary. The battle will be hard, but the victory will be yours. *"A thousand may fall at your side; ten thousand at your right hand, but it will not come near you"* (Psalm 91). Once you have crossed the Jordan, you will immediately come up against fortified strongholds of the enemy. But as Joshua marched his forces around Jericho in obedience to the command of God and the walls of the city fell, so, if you are obedient and trust in the Lord, He will cause the enemy's defences to crumble before you and He will give you victory.

Therefore the Lord says to you, be strong and very courageous. Remember that you are fully equipped. You have everything that is necessary. You are clothed with the armour that I have given you, wear it constantly and pray constantly in the spirit. I have especially equipped you with the SWORD OF THE SPIRIT, WHICH IS THE WORD OF GOD. I HAVE PLACED THIS IN YOUR HAND AS A WEIGHTY AND UN-ASSAILABLE WEAPON and you must learn to use it well. I have therefore given you all that is necessary. You are fully equipped for the task for which I have chosen and called you."

I wondered what was happening as Robin was not speaking in his usual tone; his voice had such authority. At first I thought, "What a nice thing to say" and then it hit me that God was speaking to me. The weight I could feel in my left hand wasn't a dagger, it was the sword of the spirit, His word. This was one of those awesome moments in life that you just can't put into words. After he stopped speaking, it was a while before anyone moved. Robin went and sat in his usual chair, he looked exhausted. As he leaned back, he exclaimed "That was amazing, that has never happened to me before." "Nor me" I answered. I didn't know what to do. Robin said that it was all so vivid in his mind that he would write it down for me so that I could think and pray over it.

Many years passed before I had any understanding of what this prophecy meant. I felt that it was very important to keep it to myself. It was just between God and me. Anyway, I was aware that God had a lot more to do before I would be ready for anything like this. Over the next few years He continued to bring things to the surface. Throughout this time, as well as healing the hurts and changing my attitudes, He also never stopped reassuring and confirming His word to me.

One such occasion was at Pentecost Praise at Ely Cathedral in 1991. The speaker was talking about disobedience. He used Joshua as an example and he said "What if Joshua had not crossed the Jordan and taken God's people into the Promised Land?" I felt God nudging me. The speaker closed by inviting anyone who felt God had spoken to them to come forward for prayer. What did I do? Nothing! The doubts started coming in. "It's not for you Shirley, you don't want to draw attention to yourself." I wanted to respond but fear kept holding me back. After a little while, a lady in front of me turned and said "Are you going to be obedient?" As you can imagine this shook me, so much so that initially I couldn't move, but then I slowly made my way forwards. You know God does have a sense of humour, because when I got to the front everybody else had gone and there I was all alone, the centre of attention, just what I had wanted to avoid! Thankfully, it wasn't long before one of the ladies came and took me to the rear of the cathedral for prayer. I didn't say anything to her except that I had felt God speak to me during the evening.

It's hard to describe how I felt when she started to pray for me. My whole body just started to tingle and it became stronger and stronger, and my breathing got deeper. It felt strange but wonderful. The word that was spoken over me was one God had given me many times before, Isaiah 43 v 1-4. "*I have called you by name, you are mine.*" I know that at the time I didn't fully understand exactly what it was all about. However, this I did know, God was filling and equipping me for something. As I made my way back to my seat, my legs were like jelly but I felt as if I was walking on air.

It was during this time that I had a vision of church leaders and other people walking down Huntingdon High Street, singing and praising God, in what I later realised was a "March for Jesus". As I had never had a vision before, I thought it would be best to speak to my minister. It saddened me deeply to hear from him that a "March for Jesus" would be impossible, as the division between the Catholic and Protestant churches was too great. This division, I later discovered, was to play a key part in the work to which God would call me.

Chapter Two
An invitation to Uganda

As the next few years passed, God continued to heal and restore me, but I also went through some difficult changes as one by one my friends, including Robin and Margaret, moved away. I wondered sometimes how I was going to cope without them. I didn't realise it at the time, but God was taking away my props. He was teaching me to depend on Him. It was Easter 1996 and Tony and I started to attend a little Anglican Church in a village near us called Hemingford Grey. Rev Stephen Talbot, the Priest in charge at that time and his wife Margaret were both on the WTC team. I am not into church hopping, we had been in our previous church for over 28 years, but sometimes God has a purpose in moving us around. This was definitely one of those times. It wasn't an easy time for us, change never is, but it wasn't long before we knew without doubt that this was where we were meant to be.

Two months later, a young man from Uganda came to preach one Sunday evening. His name was John Mulinde. When he first arrived in Britain, the only person he knew was Charles Mugisha, a Rwandan who was staying in Hemingford Grey. He got in touch with Charles, who encouraged him to come to the village. Charles introduced him to Stephen and asked if he could preach that Sunday night. Because Stephen had known Charles for some time and trusted his judgement, it wasn't a problem for him and he gave his permission. Little did he know what this was going to mean to us all!

John talked about life in Uganda and of the pain and suffering of his people, especially during the time of Idi Amin, and how this had left a spirit of hopelessness in the land. He knew that God longed to bring His healing, but didn't know how. So he spent many days and weeks searching the scriptures, praying, fasting and seeking God's will. God revealed to him how Abraham had walked the land in obedience to His call and everywhere he went, he set up altars of prayer and worship. He felt that God was again looking for a people to do the same. The more he prayed, the more God revealed to him. He showed him that He had a plan for Uganda long before it even existed, but the innocent blood that had been shed through the centuries had left a curse on the land for more bloodshed. There was a real need for repentance and forgiveness. So, he and others travelled around the country teaching and sharing what he felt God had given him. The people became hungry for more and that hunger led them to seek God in a new way. They made prayer a priority, both in their homes and in their churches. They also went into the bush, sometimes for days and nights, to cry out for God to come and heal their land. This was preparing the way for what God was yet to do.

As John was speaking, it was for me just as if God had switched on a light and I felt Him saying "This is it Shirley." If I had been the sort of person to shout out or jump up and down, that's what I would have done. I was so excited, as I realised prayer was the key. When John stopped speaking, a friend turned to me and said "I had a picture for you. It was of a sword and I felt God say, *This is the battle Shirley*". I found this amazing, as I remembered the sword in the prophecy God had given me six years earlier. After the service ended, I knew I had to speak to Stephen. I didn't know what I was going to say, I just knew I had to see him. I was so pleased when he said that God had been speaking to him too. We didn't know it then, but this was to be the beginning of quite an adventure.

One of the things that struck me was John's honesty. He shared personal things about his first wife, Prossey and himself, and I found it very helpful to hear how they had been challenged. He revealed how God had shown them areas in their own lives that needed to be cleansed, healed and restored. If we are to be used by God we have to let Him clear all our wrong attitudes and sin. This meant John spent long sessions alone with God, meditating on His Word and in prayer.

After a while, God started to reveal to him a prophetic word for Britain from Isaiah 60 "*Arise, shine, for your light has come and the glory of the Lord rises upon you.*" As he was praying, he saw a thick darkness that was coming from Europe and covered all the lands. A light then rose up from Britain and spread out, crossing over into Europe, pushing back the darkness as it went. He said that God had given Britain a great responsibility. Just as He had called this nation in the past to spread His Word, He now had a special purpose for us again. We were urged to take this seriously. He told us that;

1) We must be careful to move in God's timing, not ours. This means spending time seeking His will.
2) Revival comes only after long seasons of prayer.
3) God wants the land free.

Months later, I read in our church notices; "John Mulinde from the World Trumpet Mission in Uganda invites members of the church to their annual prayer and fasting conference in Kampala next January." I remember turning to Tony and saying that I would really love to go, but that was all and I forgot about it. Sometime later, I was at a prayer meeting and we were seeking to hear from God about who He wanted to send on this trip. I hadn't been there long when I felt as if God was telling me that I was going to Africa. No, Shirley, I thought, you definitely have got this wrong. My daughter Alison was due to have her second child about that time and money was a bit short as Tony, due to ill health, had been unable to work for the past 16 years. No, this had to be wishful thinking! So I said nothing. To my surprise, Stephen turned to me and said he thought God was telling me to go. He even asked if Tony would come too! When I arrived home, I shared this with Tony and to my surprise he said he wouldn't be going, but I could go if I wanted. I was shocked. It wasn't what I had expected at all. Over the next few days, God made it clear that this was His will and one of the songs we sang on the Sunday was,

"Here I am Lord, it is I Lord, I have heard you calling in the night. I will go Lord, if you lead me, I will hold your people in my heart." I knew I had to take this step of faith and trust Him.

So it wasn't a surprise when I got a phone call from Stephen telling me that the flight was booked. No going back now! The church was financing Stephen, but my friend Sylvia and I had to finance ourselves. Within a few days, I got a call to say that the bill for the flight was paid. Wow! Over the next week or two, many more contributions were given towards my expenses. God was so faithful, and He continued to make sure everything was covered.

It was very close to our departure date when I received a phone call from a church friend who had been to Uganda before. She was checking to see if we had got everything under control. As I had never flown, I was relying on others to tell me what I needed. She asked if I had the airport tax sorted, which I would have to pay when I left Uganda. She added, "It would be a good idea to have it ready in dollars." The very next day, the post arrived and with it a letter from a couple who were unaware of this phone call. They said they would be remembering us all in their prayers and enclosed was the money for the airport tax. They added that only too often, people forget this and to ensure my safe return, they thought they would send it to me in dollars! God, you are so amazing! You said that I was to trust you and you are faithful to all your promises.

I thank God often for all those who made it possible for me to go to Uganda and how He prepared me by removing all obstacles, even my fear of heights. This fear had always been a part of my life. Many times at night, I was filled with restless sleep and nightmares. I was usually looking over a cliff or falling to the ground at high speed. I got to a stage where I couldn't let this go on. It was affecting my whole life. Thankfully, because I was then on the WTC team, I had met a couple who had been willing to pray with me in the past, so I was sure they would do so again. They welcomed me with open arms and over a cup of tea, they asked me to share what the problem was. I explained about my fear of heights and how I had no idea where it had come from.

I had come to recognise that sometimes we lock away memories that we don't want to face. Agreeing to be prayed for is effectively giving the Holy Spirit permission to unlock that memory. As we sat quietly before God, suddenly the memory came flooding back. "I think I know where the problem is," I said. I went on to share how, when I was very young, my family went on a day trip to Great Yarmouth. My Dad had promised us a ride that took you around fairyland. I was so excited. We didn't have holidays or many trips out, so this was very special. Soon after we arrived, we made our way to the funfair and onto the ride. My brother, sister and I got in the first car, Mum and Dad sat behind. It wasn't long before I realised that for me this was not the fun ride my Dad had promised. We went up and up and up, then when we reached the top, I remember the fear that filled me, because right in front of us was a sheer drop. We were on the Big Dipper, a high roller-coaster ride. I started to scream and scream. I was so frightened.

As I remembered this, the tears just started to flow. I realised that this was when my fear of heights began. I had trusted my Dad to look after me and I felt he had let me down. I am sure he thought that we would all enjoy the ride, but the day that I had so looked forward to was ruined. I found it hard to believe that this had left such a mark on my life. I opened up to the Holy Spirit and allowed the love of Jesus to touch me again. I can remember even now the feeling of healing and release as I forgave my Dad. Afterwards, Jesus assured me that He was with me, then and now. When He said "*I will never leave you or forsake you*" He really meant it and "*Perfect love casts out fear*" (1 John 4 v 18). I didn't know it at the time, but God had to deal with my fear of heights to get me on that plane to Africa.

Chapter Three
Who Will Stand in the Gap?

The days and weeks seemed to fly by and soon it was the day of our departure in January 1997. I was so excited, but also very apprehensive. My first flight ever and God sends me to Africa! This must be what He meant when He said "I would travel first class."

On arrival at Entebbe Airport, the first thing that hit me was the warmth, after leaving cold old Britain behind. My heart began to race as it sank in that this was for real, we were in Africa. Sylvia and I were getting more nervous now, what had we done?

As we drove through the streets, I was amazed at how many people were still about, even though it was late. Everywhere you looked, there were people selling their goods, either from huts lit by candles, or on stools by the side of the road. It had been a long day and we were relieved when we arrived at our destination and Sylvia and I were introduced to our host, a very elegant lady named Elizabeth, or Beth for short. We were both astonished as we entered the gates and saw the beautiful home God had provided for us. I don't know what I had been expecting, but it was nothing as grand as this! The entrance hall was large and timber-lined with very impressive carved wooden doors. Sylvia and I were shown through to the part of the house where we would be staying. To our amazement, there was a bathroom with gold-coloured taps and a flushing toilet! We had been warned that the toilet might be outside, and that we would have to be careful of the cockroaches at night. We were in such a wonderful place it was hard to believe that we had been so blessed. We learned later that the home belonged to a member of the Royal Family who had lost most of their land in the time of Idi Amin.

After breakfast the next day, a car arrived to pick us up. Kampala traffic was chaotic and getting to the conference itself was quite an experience. When we arrived, we were escorted onto the stage and seated in the front row, not what we had expected. We were being treated like V.I.P.s.

The theme of the conference was "*If my people, who are called by my name, will humble themselves and pray and seek my face, and turn from their wicked ways, then will I hear from Heaven, forgive their sin and heal their land.*" (2 Chronicles 7 v 14).

The next two weeks were to be for us both challenging and humbling, as we witnessed the teaching being put into action. We saw people from many different tribes, districts and countries come together, to seek forgiveness from each other and from God, not only for what they themselves had done, but also for what their ancestors had done before them and for the innocent blood that had been shed. The stories we heard were heartbreaking and sometimes unbelievable, how could we humans do this to each other? It was a real eye-opener as we witnessed the outpouring of hearts in repentance, followed by tears of joy and laughter, African style of course, as love and forgiveness were released.

Ruby, a lady who shared our home with us, had come from Rwanda to offer her forgiveness for what had happened to her brother. He had been killed by Ugandan soldiers, right in front of her and in the most gruesome way. She felt it was important to show she had forgiven them. We found out the following year that she had died shortly after returning home. I felt it was a privilege to have met this gracious lady and to recognise that by releasing her forgiveness, she would have known such peace before she died.

Although we were touched by all the stories, it felt strange, as if it was nothing to do with us. How wrong we were. God opened our eyes to see the evidence that was all around us of the British rule during the Colonial years, as many of the large houses with huge gardens are now left empty and unattended, while the Ugandan people live in very inadequate dwellings and sometimes not even that. Despite the injustice, I was overwhelmed by how they treated us with such love and respect, and their hospitality towards us was second to none. It wasn't long before we felt God convicting us of the British arrogance and superiority, and for all that we had done over the centuries to our African brothers and sisters. At the conference that evening, we asked if we could follow their example and address this issue by asking their forgiveness.

John thanked us and went on to say that despite the damage that was done during this period of time, we had to remember God had used Britain to bring them the Gospel. This is something they will always be thankful for, even though they now ask the question, "What has happened to Britain?" They then passed us the Union Jack flag and a prophetic word was spoken over us for our country. They declared that God would touch the United Kingdom so that it would once again become the land that spreads the Gospel throughout the world. I felt someone tug on my arm, it was one of the leaders. He pulled me back and I felt a little worried. I thought that I had done something wrong, but he only wanted to ask if he could pray with me. He said "God says He will lead you where He wants you to go, just be obedient." And once again I was reminded of Esther 4 v 14.

One of the most significant times for us was the President of Uganda's visit to the conference. Security was very tight and there were armed guards everywhere. There was an air of excitement around as we waited for the President to arrive. After the introductions, John gave an overview of what the conference was all about. He then thanked the President for all he had done to bring peace and prosperity to their country. In his reply, the president graciously received the thanks and said that although his wife was a Christian, he himself at that time did not hold the same view. However, he had to acknowledge that prayer had made a difference in the land! He told us that many years ago, he had been involved with Scripture Union and that he did have a good knowledge of the Bible.

After he had spoken, John thanked him for his kind words. He then proceeded to ask if the President would hand the flag of Uganda over to the conference, as a sign of handing the nation back to God. He agreed, and so in front of us all, and on national television, he handed the flag over. As he did this, I felt God say to me, "What you see Me do here, I can do where you are too." I could hardly move, and the tears started to flow. What was God saying? After the National Anthem, the president left and the atmosphere was electric. We were all amazed at what we had just witnessed. The worship was so joyful, we just wanted to praise God for what He had done.

One thing we all recognised while we were in Uganda was that we had much to learn from these very dedicated people. They knew repentance and humility of a depth that we were yet to learn, and there was a power in their prayers that we, at that time, could only dream of. We asked God to teach us more and through the things we witnessed and the teaching from John and others, that's exactly what God did.

During my time in Uganda, 2 Chronicles 7 v 14 took on a new meaning for me. Our WTC teaching helped us to understand that just as individuals need sins forgiven, wounds healed and to be set free from wrong attitudes, so do families, tribes, churches, villages, towns and even nations. Injustice or innocent bloodshed needs to be addressed. In Uganda, we had seen it put into practice.

The first word in 2 Chronicles 7 v 14 is "If". It all depends on us being willing. God longs to heal our land, but we must do our bit, to humble ourselves and bring everything before Him. Then He will show us what is in our own lives, as well as the land, that needs His divine touch.

All too soon it was time to leave Uganda. We were all very tired and longed to get home to our families, but, we were also sad to be leaving these lovely people. Once home, we quickly slipped back into our normal routine. However, I was often awake at night as I found I wanted to spend more time in prayer. On one of these occasions that I felt God giving me this word:

My land is crying out
Who will care?
Who will stand in the gap?
Will you?

My people are destroying themselves, breaking hearts,
Who will cry for them?
Who will stand in the gap?
Will you?

Babies are murdered, children abused, sickness and suicides
Who will care?
Who will cry?
Who will stand in the gap?
Will you?

I want to heal, I want to restore,
I want to bring new hope and new beginnings
Who will care?
Who will cry?
Who will stand in the gap?
Will you?

I felt this was a challenge not only to me but also to all God's people.
We need to cry out to God on behalf of our own nations.

Chapter Four

God's Redemptive Purpose

As the days and weeks passed, Africa seemed like a dream. However, it was good to share our stories with churches or groups in the area. It was evident to us all that people were really interested and wanted to know more than time allowed. We soon realised that we needed to set up a forum where not only our stories could be heard, but also the principles we had learnt could be taught.

Stephen had already been thinking along the lines of setting up a conference in Huntingdon, so he got in touch with John Mulinde to see if he would come over to England in May 1997 and do a weekend of teaching for us. We knew this man had an anointing on him and we wanted to give more people an opportunity to hear what God had done in his life, as well as in his land. Besides, we wanted to hear more ourselves.

After months of planning, the day arrived and we were honoured to have the then Bishop of Huntingdon, the Rt Rev John Flack, open the conference. It meant a lot to have his encouragement and to know that someone in authority was supporting us. Over the weekend, my heart stirred within me as the name of Jesus was lifted high and Christians from so many different denominations came together to praise our Lord. Again, I was reminded of Psalm 133, "*How good and pleasant it is when brothers live together in unity—for there the Lord bestows his blessing, even life forevermore.*"

John's theme for the conference was "Remember your Prophetic Destiny", using Jeremiah 29 v 11, "*For I know the plans I have for you, plans to prosper you and not to harm you, plans to give you hope and a future. Then you will call upon me and pray to me, and I will listen to you. You will seek me and find me when you seek me with all your heart.*" He went on to explain what he meant by this:

1) Look back into the past and see what has affected you for good and bad.
2) As we recognise the traumas in our lives, we can see what God needs to do to bring reconciliation and healing. It is then that we will also recognise what things have happened within God's church over past years which have never been healed.
3) We must allow God to highlight areas of wrong attitudes and unforgiveness.
4) We need to be working together, increasingly reaching out across denominations to show how much we need each other, building HIS Church instead of our own, so that no man shall boast.

John shared how we needed to take responsibility for what our own people group has done. He said that if we don't deal with the past, the past will catch up with us, whether that is in our family, church, area or even our nation. We each represent our own particular group, for example, the denomination we belong to, our families, the place where we live, as well as our nation. He said that when we go to speak to people with all the love of Jesus, the chances are they will not see Him, they will see what was done in the past. Even as we speak the words to them, they are looking for the hidden meaning, wondering why we would say such things. God wants to heal such thinking.

John then asked, what is God's redemptive purpose for you? He shared how God has a purpose for each and every one of us, and how He also has a plan for Huntingdon and Huntingdonshire. What is that purpose? Are we still fulfilling it? If not, what went wrong? This made the hairs on the back of my neck stand on end. The connection with what John was saying and how I had been thinking was unbelievable. As he researched our area, he discovered that in 1799, the Church Missionary Society was started in Huntingdonshire by John Venn, son of Rev Henry Venn, Rector of Yelling. Huntingdon had also played a key role in the beginning of aviation, and that the idea of what we now know as parliamentary democracy was birthed in the heart of Oliver Cromwell, a son of Huntingdon. It was as if we were being shown that in the past, we had been used to birth new things. Yet if you spoke to anyone and asked what they thought of Huntingdon, they would very likely say "It's dead." This wasn't right, we believed it was the opposite of what God intended for the area and it made us eager to look into history for ourselves, to see what we could find that may have caused this change.

It's amazing what you discover when you start delving into history, things that have caused division between people that still affects us today. Take Cromwell for example. I am ashamed to say that I knew nothing about him apart from the fact that he had been born in Huntingdon. I was to learn that he had been brought up with a strong faith in God and that he was a Puritan and therefore had strong views on idolatry. For him, this idolatry was found mostly in the Catholic faith. This belief affected him deeply and the part he was to play in the English Civil War during the 17th Century.

It wasn't long after this that my son returned home very concerned about a problem that was causing division between certain churches in our town. The next day, my telephone rang quite early; it was a friend who was working some distance away. She said "You are never going to believe this Shirley, but I am standing in a muddy field in the middle of Sussex, thinking about Huntingdon." She went on to say that on the way there that morning, she had been thinking and praying about the Civil War and felt God say that it wasn't just a civil war, it was a religious war. This really started me thinking, had this war affected us? Also, what was behind the division in the churches, was it something we had done? Or was it something we had inherited? Or maybe even both?

We have always recognised the good that Cromwell achieved. However, it is also obvious that much was done during the Civil War that was unjust and brought division and disunity. Some 20 ministers in Huntingdonshire alone were imprisoned in Huntingdon jail. They were badly treated and many lost their livelihoods, and some even their lives, for bowing the knee and having a communion rail, which the Puritans believed to be idolatrous. Many families were divided during this part of England's history, brother against brother, father against son. Whole families were torn apart, one side supporting King Charles I, the other Cromwell. The more I thought about this war, the more it bothered me. I realised that it was led by someone from my people group (from Huntingdon) and also it had been done in the name of Christ. This meant that it was Christian against Christian, Protestant against Catholic, as well as family against family. This would cause a deep root of division and pain, and as I was to find out later, not only in England but also across into Ireland, and beyond. Without a doubt, it had affected many people and the wound was so deep that the effects still continue. It was like a cancer of bitterness and division that has been handed down from generation to generation.

Are we reaping the division that was sown into our land all those years ago? The Bible says in Galatians 6 v 7, "*Do not be deceived, God cannot be mocked. A man reaps what he sows.*" There are always consequences for sin, either your own, your family's, your church's, your town's or your nation's. If we doubt this at all, we only have to go back in scripture to see what happened to the nation of Israel. In Hosea 10 v 12-13, God says to his people "*Sow for yourself righteousness; reap the fruit of unfailing love, and break up your unploughed ground, for it is time to seek the Lord, until he showers righteousness on you. But you have planted wickedness and have reaped evil; you have eaten the fruit of deception.*" I remembered John's words that if you don't deal with the past, it will catch up with you.

The second very important thing that came out of the conference was the need to encourage unity by gathering people from all denominations to pray for our area. We recognised that many were already praying in their own churches, but both Stephen and I felt God was saying that we must unite and seek His purpose together to bring revival to our land. After all, is this unity not what Jesus prayed for just before He died? Stephen shared the vision of a prayer gathering with local ministers and it wasn't long before we began a monthly meeting of praise and prayer. *Prayer for Huntingdonshire* had been born!

The third thing we felt very strongly was the need to encourage people to pray for their own town/village. We had no idea how to do this, so a meeting was called for anyone who might be interested. It was here that I met Annette Quail, and to my delight, it was obvious that she had a desire to see a prayer cell in her own village. She has a real love for the place and the people, so she readily agreed to be responsible for starting a group. This was to be the beginning of a special friendship of which you will read much more.

After this meeting, we produced a leaflet to help people understand what the prayer cells were about;

1) What is a Prayer Cell? It is a group of Christians of any denomination who come together to draw closer to God and each other and catch the vision for revival in their village/town.

2) How do we function? We meet regularly, e.g. weekly or monthly.

3) Research your area's history and discern what the purpose of God was for the area. Has this purpose been fulfilled? If not, what went wrong?

4) Look at what is happening now and see where sin, e.g. disobedience, pride etc. has come in and given the enemy a foothold.

5) What is in control of the area? It could be drug addiction, freemasonry, sexual immorality, disunity, or destruction etc.

6) What has been done to corrupt God's will in this place? We need to repent and stand in the gap for past sins.

Pray against anything that is in control of the area or person and pray in the opposite, e.g. control out, freedom in; disobedience out, obedience in; pride out, humility in.

Remember what Jesus said, *"Assuredly I say to you, whatever you bind on earth will be bound in heaven, and whatever you loose on earth will be loosed in Heaven. Again I say to you, that if two of you agree on earth concerning anything that they ask, it will be done for them by my Father in Heaven."* Matthew 18 v 18-19.

Stephen and I realised that we had been very fortunate to have the teaching of *Wholeness Through Christ* in our background. This helped tremendously towards our understanding of what John Mulinde had taught. We both felt it was important to pass this on, so it became our priority to include some teaching in our monthly meetings. God was very gracious to us at this time. None of us really knew what we were doing. All we knew was that God wanted us to draw His people together to pray in unity. As many people already had a heart to see God move in this area, the prayer cells and monthly gatherings just helped to pull them together.

It was while we were at a Praise and Prayer meeting that we met Katie Sims, a tall, striking-looking lady from the local Catholic Church. Katie had been quite nervous about coming that evening. She had heard that we had been praying for someone to join us from the Catholic faith, but wasn't sure whether she would fit in. Those fears were soon dispelled! That evening, we spent time talking and praying together. We were all totally amazed when she told us that her grandfather on her father's side had been the Town Clerk of Drogheda, the first town Cromwell had taken in Ireland. She went on to say that it had also been her home for a time and some of her relatives still lived there. What an amazing link! I invited Katie round for coffee. I felt it was important for her to know the background. As I began to tell her the story, it was obvious that Katie could see the significance of why God had drawn her in and she became more and more excited. Before she left that day, she made a commitment to stand with me, as we seek to bring God's healing to a broken land.

The next few months seemed to slip by so quickly and it was hard sometimes to find time to do research. However, while I was looking around a local shop, I spotted a book on the Civil War. As I glanced through, I was horrified to read the account of Cromwell's attack on Drogheda. The more I read, the more it shook me. In letters written in his own hand, he cursed the Irish people. You could hear the underlying hatred towards the Catholics that had been handed down to him from his forefathers. (One of Cromwell's distant relatives was Thomas Cromwell, an adviser to King Henry VIII, who presided over the Dissolution of the Monasteries.) It disturbed me deeply how places like Drogheda, Wexford and many others had suffered. I am well aware that this was a time of war, but many innocent people died too. Even today, the controversy goes on about the rights and wrongs of both sides during this time. However, what I can't get passed is that this was done in the name of Christ. Priests, men, women and children were driven from their homes, their land taken from them, and thousands were killed. Not just because they were in the wrong place at the wrong time, but because they belonged to a people group called Irish Catholics. Christ died because He loves everyone equally, and to bring life and reconciliation, not death and division. I suddenly felt ashamed to come from Cromwell's hometown.

This was the starting point for me. I knew I had to go to Ireland. So, you can imagine my surprise when a few months later, in January 1998, I found myself with Stephen and Annette, back in Uganda!

Chapter Five

Uganda to Ireland

The Ugandan conference had grown since the previous year. John had travelled to many places and as a result, had invited many leaders and friends from all around the world. Some had come with music ministries, others to work with the children, and many, like Stephen, came to teach and share God's word. But why were Annette and I there? Yes, it was wonderful to be back and meet up with old friends and make new ones like Beth's brother, Prince Daniel Kjumba, who owned the beautiful house where we stayed in Kampala. We also very much enjoyed the teaching of Tom Hess, Peter Boss, Cindy Jacobs and many more, but somehow we felt we were in the wrong place. We couldn't see why God had brought us all this way to Africa, when we felt sure we should have been going to Ireland. Had we got it wrong?

All of a sudden, it became clear. It was about five days before we were due to leave and we were sitting in the Visitors Room taking a break. A man sitting next to me turned, and in a strong Irish accent asked, "What are you doing here Shirley?" I told him that I had been at the Prayer and Fasting Conference the previous year and that we had been invited back, although I wasn't entirely sure why I had returned, because I had a real desire to go to Ireland. I went on to tell him how God had been speaking to me about Cromwell's actions over there and the need for healing and reconciliation.

As I turned to look at him, I saw he had tears in his eyes. He said, "I have waited years to hear someone say that." He went on to tell me that God had been speaking to him about the Cromwell issue for some time and he felt called to retrace Cromwell's steps. He then said "Shirley, you have got to come and do it with me." My heart seemed to miss a beat. I knew that this was one of those moments in life when it had to be God. I had come all the way to Africa to meet someone with the same desire to heal this part of history. Only God could make that happen! At that moment, Stephen came into the room and I called him over. Bill and Stephen got on really well from the start and before long we were invited over to Ireland. I knew this was why we were in Uganda!

The rest of that day we couldn't help but marvel at what God was doing. All too soon, it was evening and time for Bill to leave and catch his flight home. We said our goodbyes and he said that he would be in touch. It didn't dawn on us at the time, but we didn't know his full name or where he was from, and he didn't know ours. However, we needn't have worried! Two days later, the three of us were on our way to Gaba (in Uganda's Central Region) when Stephen remembered that we hadn't confirmed our flights home. The driver said this wasn't a problem, as the communication centre was just up the road. So, we went in and made our telephone call. We were just about to leave, when a voice called "There is a fax for you, Pastor Stephen". Who could it be? Nobody knows we are here. Communication in Uganda wasn't the best, so we were astonished that this fax came through while we were there. The fax was from Bill Roy in Carrickfergus, Northern Ireland, inviting us over to join their March for Jesus and informing Stephen how to contact him! God, You are so amazing!

That evening, as we sang of the Father's love, the presence of God was tangible, but I could only watch as many around me were touched and in tears. What's wrong with me? I thought, why am I feeling so strange? I have just had this amazing time with Bill Roy and I knew that God was in that encounter, yet I stand here untouched. I still struggled with the idea that God loves me unconditionally. Was I to ever get beyond this point? We started to sing "God will make a way where there seems to be no way. He works in ways we cannot see, He will make a way for me." I just broke down in tears. A member of the music team came over, took my hand and gave me a hug. Without knowing anything, she said

"That's from Father God." Later, she told me that she had been given a picture of two roses, one white that stood for purity, and one red that stood for the blood of Christ. It also had two nasty thorns and these were for sharing in the suffering. There's the rose again! Jesus never said the road would be easy, but with the Lord's reassurance, I felt I could face anything.

In the days that followed our return home, I reflected on what had happened over the past two weeks. I pondered why I had to go all the way to Africa to meet Bill when we live relatively close. The answer came, "The Heavens aren't open here." This made me think again of the first conference in Uganda and the text "*If my people, who are called by my name, will humble themselves and pray and seek my face and turn from their wicked ways, then will I hear from Heaven, forgive their sin and heal their land.*" The conference was all about coming together in prayer, seeking God's face and forgiveness. God says that if we do these things then He will hear from Heaven and forgive our sin and heal our land. This is what I believed God was calling me to do in Ireland. I must be prepared to say I am sorry and stand in the gap for Huntingdon, the place where Cromwell was born and brought up. It says in Ezekiel 22 v 30 that God looked for a man among them to stand in the gap. It couldn't be Ezekiel himself as he was in exile, it had to be someone from that place, but He found no one. God had called me and as I am from Huntingdon, I knew I could stand in the gap.

Over the weeks that followed, God continued to give us confirmation of His desire to deal with this bitter root. On one occasion, Stephen was asked if he would help with a WTC course in Ireland. Everything went according to plan and afterwards a lady asked if she could talk with him. She said that she came from a Catholic background and while he was sharing about Cromwell, anger rose up from deep inside her. She had had no idea that it was there, it had been hidden so deeply, but she now wanted to be free of it.

This didn't only affect Ireland of course. A friend of ours was at a barbecue in Huntingdon. She was most surprised when one of the ladies present said that the atmosphere in Huntingdon was so heavy and that she wouldn't be surprised if it didn't go way back to Cromwell! We are not saying that everything is Cromwell's fault, but we do recognise that during this part of English history, many unrighteous things were done and innocent blood was shed. What makes it worse was that it was done in the name of Christ. This opened the door for yet more violence to follow, as the Bible says in Hosea 4 v 2-3 "*Bloodshed follows bloodshed, and because of this, the land mourns.*" When Cain killed Abel, God said in Genesis 4 v 10 "*Your brother's blood cries out to me from the ground.*"

One day out of the blue, Stephen asked me if I would go to Belfast and represent our area in the "March for Jesus". I must admit, I was a little surprised, as nothing had been said for a while. He told me that he had only just heard from Bill Roy and felt it was important for someone from Huntingdon to go. I agreed. He asked if I thought Annette might like to go too. Annette and I had got to know each other well while we were in Uganda, and I saw a side of her that touched me deeply. She had a gentle, humble spirit that often brought her to tears as she saw the injustice. I had no problem asking her to join me, especially as her husband comes from Belfast.

Unfortunately, the morning we were due to fly, I awoke feeling unwell with tonsillitis. I didn't want to miss this trip, so I packed myself off with plenty of tablets. We came in to land at Belfast and the weather was wet and miserable. I was a bit disappointed as this was my first visit to Ireland. However, it was good to see Bill Roy again and catch up on what had been happening since we met in Uganda.

Bill and several church leaders arrived early the next morning for a prayer meeting. They told us that the walk had four different starting points, north, south, east and west of Belfast. The plan was that each group would set off at the same time and arrive together in front of St Anne's Cathedral, where there would be a service at which Christian Lodewyck from South Africa would speak.

I don't know what I expected to see as we walked the streets that afternoon. It's so easy to get the wrong impression of Ireland from what you see on the television. Yes, we saw murals on the walls that spoke of violence and soldiers on street corners with their guns ready for any trouble. However, we also saw children playing, and ordinary people getting on with their lives, trying to live peacefully. There was a wonderful sense of unity when we got to the Cathedral as people descended from all directions and greeted one another. We felt very privileged to be there.

That evening, our hosts arranged for us to attend a meeting they had seen advertised which was led by a team from the United States. The talk was based on Esther 4 v 14; "*who knows but that you have come to royal position for such a time as this.*" I was still feeling unwell, so it was difficult to concentrate, but I was very encouraged by the fact that this verse which was given to me many years ago was used. When the speaker had finished, he invited people up for prayer. Although I am not good at this, I was feeling so ill I just wanted someone to pray with me. As I waited my turn, I couldn't help but notice how each person was ministered to in a gentle loving way but also with such power. A gentleman walked towards me and before I could say anything, he said, "I can see a crown being put on your head, it's the crown of a princess." Although I had wanted to tell him about my throat, I knew that what he was saying was important, so I just kept quiet and listened. He went on, "No, it isn't a princess - it's a crown of authority. God says to you "Things do not have to stay the same, when you speak, things will change, for you will speak with His authority". This was an awesome moment for me. I knew that there was a connection between the scripture used that night and the words spoken over me now. I wasn't sure what it was, but I knew it was from God. I sat down feeling rather stunned and was glad that nobody asked me any questions. Once we were back in our room, I was able to share with Annette what had happened. Looking again at Esther 4 v 14, we knew straight away that we were being encouraged to spend more time in prayer, fasting and waiting on God.

After a good night's sleep, we joined the fellowship at Gateway Church in Carrickfergus. I was feeling better and looking forward to hearing Christian Lodewyck speak. He shared some of the amazing story of how God used him in South Africa to bring about reconciliation. When he finished, he invited people forward, "I'm not anyone special," he said, "but what God has given me and what I have experienced, I would like to pass on to you." Once more, I was reluctant to make a move. I felt that this was for the Irish people, not me. I was wrong. The music started to play and nearly everyone had moved to the front, including Annette, when I too felt compelled to join them too.

The tears started to well up within me as I listened to the music. Christian Lodewyck came towards me and laid his hand on my head. He said in a gentle voice, "After today you will never doubt again what God has called you to do. God is going to increase your faith." I just stood as tears ran down my face. I knew we were in the presence of God. The song being sung was, "No one else in history is like you, for history itself belongs to you. Alpha and Omega you have loved me, and I will share eternity with you. It's all about you, Jesus, and all this is for you, for your glory and your fame. It's not about me, as if you should do things my way, you alone are God and I surrender to your ways." I didn't move. I just wanted to stay in God's presence.

We were sad to say goodbye, but we were sure it wouldn't be long before we would return. At the airport, we checked in at the desk and went off to have a cup of tea. Before we had even got to the café, Annette heard our names being called over the loudspeakers. We rushed back, thinking there must be a problem with our luggage. We could see a very long queue as we approached the desk. We were directed to the front and the attendant started to apologise to us, because apparently we should have been first-class passengers! We were so surprised! Did they really mean us, Annette Quail and Shirley Bowers, travelling first-class? I suddenly remembered those words given to me all those years ago; "You are going to travel first-class." I knew straight away that God was showing me that the connection between Huntingdon (known as Cromwell country) and Ireland was one He wanted me to make.

We were given a card that allowed us into the first-class lounge where we felt a little out of place! We were escorted onto the plane and as we took off, Annette said, "Everywhere is so green, you can see why this is called the "Emerald Isle." It was a wonderful journey, being pampered with a three-course meal, hot towels and the most comfortable seats. It made us feel like royalty! We were so excited as we recalled what Christian Lodewyck had prayed over me that morning; "After today you will never doubt again what God has called you to do and He is going to increase your faith." He had certainly done that! I needed to dig out my WTC papers, and find the one about the first-class travel. I wanted to see what else God had said to me that day.

The next day, I eagerly rummaged through all my paper work. It was with excitement that I reread the scriptures given to me, and it struck me how soon we forget the promises God makes to us. I read the bit about how I was in a boat, and was lifted out with a net, and God said no, this isn't right. You are going to travel first-class! At the bottom of the page, it had PTO. I turned it over and on the other side was written, "Picture of a green place and God said, "Never mind your enemies, we are going to have a picnic!" I remembered what Annette had said about Ireland being called the Emerald Isle, a green place.

Sometime later, I was sharing all this with my son Jonathan. He looked at me with a smile saying "Do you realise what you just said Mum?" I must have looked puzzled because he went on, "Repeat the picture that the lady gave to you." So I did. "I was in a boat and I was lifted out with **a net**, and God said no, this isn't right, you are going to travel first-class." Then it hit me, not only did he give me a first-class ticket, but I was with **Annette**! Wow! How amazing! I couldn't have made it up! I realised that God wanted Annette to know that she was very much part of His plan too.

Chapter Six
The Spotlight

The months that followed were spent prayer walking around the villages in Cambridgeshire, encouraging others in prayer. Annette and I spent quite a bit of time back in my home village of Warboys. Although I had lived there for the first twenty years of my life, I never really knew anything about its history until I started to read the true story of the Warboys witches.

In 1540, Richard Cromwell (Oliver's uncle) owned much of the land around Ramsey including The Manor House, next to Warboys Church. Later, the house was rented a family and Alice Samuel worked there as a housekeeper. Alice was accused of witchcraft and a confession was forced from her. As a result, and she, her husband and her child were all hanged on Huntingdon market square on 7th April, 1593. It was later proven that they were innocent, but too late. This was an unjust act, as many were in those days, but that doesn't make it right. Three innocent lives were lost. God desires justice and holiness and I pray that one day true repentance for this wrong will come from that village.

People have said to me "It's only history; it doesn't make any difference now." Well, if that's the case, then why do we let it live on, as though it's a joke? The children of Warboys wear a badge with a witch on a broomstick on their school blazers. I, like many from the village, pray that one day it will be replaced with something that both the children and the village can be proud of.

Take my advice. Research your history and see what has happened that still affects your town. Was it good, or was it bad? Is it something you can praise God for, or something you need to bring before Him in repentance?

All through this time, God was gracious to me and on many

occasions, He would remind me of what He had called me to do. I remember one day in particular when I received a letter from a lady in Dublin named Dr Janet Craven. I didn't know it then, but Janet had a sister in St Ives, a town not far from Huntingdon. I had never met Janet, yet she had heard all about me and wondered if I had anyone in Ireland praying for me on a regular basis. She said that she felt that retracing Cromwell's steps was so important that she would love to do this, and get others to pray too. I can't tell you how this made me feel this lady who, I was to learn, had been a missionary in Africa for years, felt called to pray for me. I wondered what had I done to deserve this. The answer to that question is, of course, that I hadn't done anything, but it is all of God. Anyway, I was so touched and amazed that when I sent details to her, I asked if we could meet next time she was over in Huntingdonshire. We have met on many occasions now, one of which you will read about later.

It had been an unforgettable year and it was now November and the days were growing shorter and darker. As I was reflecting back over the year and thanking God for His faithfulness, I had a picture/vision of a spotlight. I didn't understand what this meant, but felt God saying "Get into the spotlight Shirley, for I am with you." What could this mean? I certainly wasn't the type of person, who wanted to be noticed, so what could God be saying?

My thoughts started to return to Ireland, and I wondered what was going on over there. That same week, while we were at one of the prayer gatherings, someone felt God saying to me, "Don't hold back. Trust me." I had a very uncomfortable feeling. Was God calling me back to Ireland? I just didn't know. I wish I didn't doubt so easily, I thought. At this time, I was reading Genesis 15 and in verse 8 it says, "*Abram said, O Sovereign Lord, how can I know?*" And God replies "*I will give you a sign.*" I thought if this great man of faith needed assurance that he was doing God's will, then it's OK for me to need reassurance too! I can't tell you how relieved I felt!

When our group next met for prayer, I was surprised when someone said "What are you doing about Ireland, Shirley?" I hadn't told anyone what I had been feeling. "You have got to go back you know," she went on "and you need to get it organised soon". I then shared some of what had happened that week, but I still didn't tell anyone about the spotlight.

Christmas came and went and nothing seemed to happen to point the way. One Sunday in January, I went with Annette to the evening service at her church. The Pastor preached on how the Holy Spirit is like a spotlight that shines on areas that need attention. I couldn't believe my ears, I knew this wasn't a coincidence; this had to be God speaking to me. Later I showed Annette what I had written in my Bible about the spotlight vision and asked her to pray with me. Afterwards, I said to her that I might get in touch with Bill Roy in Carrickfergus, to ask if he felt it right for me to come over to Ireland again. Almost immediately, I changed my mind. If God wanted this to happen, I wasn't going to interfere.

Fortunately, God didn't keep me waiting long. The next day, a letter arrived from Bill Roy, asking if I would attend a meeting the following week! Leaders of churches from all over Ireland were coming together to seek God and the way forward. He also invited me to a conference in May with Irish politicians and other leaders. He enclosed a leaflet. I couldn't believe my eyes, for on the front cover was a picture of a stage with a spotlight shining on it! I have kept the leaflet as a constant reminder that this is God's work and although He uses us, it is by His grace that I am able to do anything.

The day after, I visited one of the Prayer Cells and met up again with Katie Sims. They wanted to pray with me before I left for Ireland. They did something that at that time I hadn't come across before, called prophetic intercession. As they prayed, they covered me with a purple flag and then a red one, and spoke over me the words; "Do not be afraid, I am going with you, I have placed on you, my daughter, a royal robe and you are protected by my blood. You go in my authority. I am going to do something in your day that will amaze you." I was pretty amazed already how much more could there be?

The next week, I flew to Ireland by myself for the first time. How I marvelled at what God had done for me, not long ago I would never have flown at all, let alone travel on my own. Gateway Church is an old converted warehouse and it was named Gateway as it faces the estuary, the shipping entrance to Northern Ireland. After a time of worship, Bill introduced me and I was invited to say a few words, after which they all were invited to pray for me. As they prayed, I was astounded as God confirmed His word to me. Someone had a picture of me being robed from head to foot in red silk. They went on, "I feel the Lord is saying, you are going into enemy ground, deeper than ever before and I am protecting you with my blood." I remembered the red flag that had been put on me before I left England. Someone else had a picture of a bunch of keys, "The Lord has given you the keys, Shirley, to unlock what the enemy has done, you have His authority to smash the gates of Hell." At this point I hadn't a clue what lay ahead of me, only God knew. By His grace, He had used people both in Ireland and in England to help prepare the way.

The following day, I was invited to an interdenominational prayer group. It was a pleasure to be in a place where Protestants and Catholics met together in freedom from any fear. They shared some of their experiences of the troubles in Northern Ireland, especially around the time of the marching season. The marching season is a time, mainly in July, when some Protestant Unionists parade through the streets to commemorate centuries-old military victories, often passing through volatile Catholic areas. They told me how ordinary people, who normally live in peace, suddenly turn on one another. Lives, as well as homes, were threatened and this wasn't only something they heard about on the news, some of them had experienced it personally. I was only just beginning to understand how hard it has been for the folk there. I still believed that what Cromwell had done in this land had had a huge effect, but I didn't understand why, as I was in Northern Ireland and he went to the Republic. I needed to do more research. As we continued in prayer, I asked the Lord and the people there to forgive the hurt we had caused through Cromwell and also to show any wrong attitude in our own hearts. Afterwards, a Catholic lady came and thanked me, "When you began to pray, I became very angry. I didn't realise at first what the problem was. Then, suddenly, it was as if God lit a candle and I could see my life clearly. Ever since I can remember, I have had a deep anger and bitterness in my heart towards Cromwell, but I had no understanding of why." She went on, "I asked God to forgive me and set me free from this and I know the anger and the bitterness has gone." Praise the Lord!

On the Saturday, leaders from all over Ireland came together. It was here I met Ian Bothwell. Ian and his wife, Pauline, run an organisation called "Crossfire Trust" near Crossmaglen, on the border. The Trust was set up to serve the broken people from the community, Protestant and Catholic. I was very impressed with this man's servant heart as he shared some of the hard times he had gone through. As I shared my story, he said to me "Do you realise that some of my neighbours wouldn't want to speak to you because you come from Cromwell's home town? They hate him so much for what he did over here." I hadn't realised that the feelings ran so deep; it was all still a steep learning curve.

On my return, I spent a great deal of time researching the history of Cromwell, particularly in Ireland. I could see that he believed he was doing the right thing by avenging the bloodshed that had been reported in the North. However, God also showed me similar stories in the Bible, for example, Genesis 34 talks of revenge and murder by Jacob's sons, Simeon and Levi, for the rape of their sister. The desire for justice was right, but their means of achieving it was wrong as many innocent people died. As a result, their father Jacob cursed them on his deathbed (Genesis 49 v 5-7) and much later, their descendants lost the land that had been promised to them. After all, Paul says in Romans 12 v 19 *"Do not take revenge my friends, but leave room for God's wrath, for it is written "It is mine to avenge, I will repay"* says the Lord".

That year, Huntingdon celebrated the 400th anniversary of Oliver Cromwell's birth. This caused some controversy as not everyone wanted to remember this date. Cromwell is often called "Huntingdon's most famous son" which makes him quite a tourist attraction, so plans were made for a big celebration. Stephen and the Team Rector of Huntingdon became very aware of the pain this planned celebration was causing our Catholic brothers and sisters. Whilst we knew that their pain was too important to be ignored, we were unsure of the way forward, so we spent many days in prayer, seeking God for His healing. You can imagine our relief when we heard that the Town Council had taken on board people's feelings and were going to tone down the events! Over the next few months, many lectures and displays took place across the town, and this was an opportunity to do more research. While in the Cromwell Museum, we noticed the motto on the Cromwell Coat of Arms in Latin, which means "Peace through war". We thought how ironic this was for a man who is remembered for his role in the Civil War. Can peace come no other way?

My next visit to Ireland, the spotlight conference, was drawing closer. Although I had got used to going places on my own, I was delighted when Annette informed me that she was taking time off work so that she could come too.

The conference turned out to be a very interesting time indeed and it was a gathering of those experienced in prayer, as well as politicians. It was interesting to hear a political perspective of what was going on in the country and to hear the different sides debated. One politician said that "If the Christians wanted to make a difference, they need to get out into the community, even if it meant moving house." I couldn't help but think of Ian and Pauline Bothwell at Crossfire Trust as this is exactly what they had done.

Later back in Carrickfergus, Annette and I were having coffee, when John Mulinde joined us. He shared some of the amazing things that had been happening in Uganda. For example, witchdoctors were being broken of their power, because the people had turned away from them and were now putting their faith in Jesus. As a result, many witchdoctors had turned to Christ too. Tribes in the North were also coming to know Jesus in their hundreds, mainly because they could feel the love and forgiveness offered to them from the tribes in South and Central Uganda. They had thought that the crimes they had committed in the past were beyond forgiveness by anyone. They were astonished that in their great need, Christians from around Uganda had sent gifts of food and clothes. What love!

Excited and inspired by what John had shared with us, we told him how God had revealed to us the reconciliation work that needed to be done about the Cromwellian part of Irish history and our role in this. I wanted to know what he thought, as someone who had been involved in this sort of prayer and reconciliation before. He told us that he believed Cromwell was still the key issue in the process of redeeming Ireland, as well as England, for God. He went on, "I would say it goes even further afield than that."

The following day, Bill invited us to go with him to a Catholic Charismatic conference in Dublin where he was one of the speakers. We were delighted as we had come from Cromwell country and we wanted to bless what God was doing in the Catholic Church. We met some lovely people in Dublin and Sister Ann Mary was one of them. When she heard of our plan to retrace the steps of Cromwell, she was greatly encouraged and blessed us for wanting to help bring healing to this land that she loves so much. She took great delight in filling us in on yet more of what had happened when Cromwell and his men invaded. She told us how thousands had been dispossessed and forced over to Galway, in the West of Ireland. She described how the Catholics were herded across the river and many lost their lives in the water, or were killed if they tried to escape. "This pain still lives on today in the people there" she added.

On the Sunday morning at Carrickfergus, Pastor Rubens Cunha Jr shared the most amazing stories of what was happening in his native Brazil; stories of people being healed, lives restored and thousands giving their lives to the Lord. We were all listening intently when a speaker that was fixed to the wall fell and knocked him unconscious! Thankfully a doctor was in the service, so we prayed while he attended to him. Amazingly, as soon as he came round, he got straight to his feet and with blood running down his face, he said "I will not be stopped from sharing the good news of what God has done," and he continued to speak for another fifteen minutes! He then prayed with people for another hour.

I was touched by this man's humility as well as his courage, so I too went up for a blessing. When he came to me, he said "God has placed into your hands a ball of fire, the Lord is giving you the power to heal, the power to heal nations." I was quite shocked. I hadn't thought of this going any further than Ireland and I still didn't feel that I had anything special that God could use. However, I did believe this was from God. Please understand that I struggled for some time before I decided to share this, as well as some of the other stories and words spoken over me. However, I want everyone to see that this is God's story. Later, when you read how things came together, I hope you too will see this.

Chapter Seven
Footprints of Blessing

The months soon passed and before we knew it, Stephen and I were back in Ireland, this time for the "Footprints of Blessing" walk which John and Yvonne Presdee had organised. They and others had already been walking for five weeks when we joined them for the last lap. We met many people during this time who affected our lives, both Christians and non-Christians. One was Phyllis Forsythe from Omagh, Northern Ireland, who became a very dear friend and prayer partner. John and Yvonne must have worked really hard to bring folk from all over Ireland, as well as other nations, to take part in this walk. Despite being tired and having sore feet, we all got on so well. We were never short of a laugh! However, it is only God who could gather people together from so many different walks of life and bring such a sense of unity and fellowship that was unforgettable. I have no doubt that if you asked anyone on the walk, they would tell you stories of how they were both challenged and blessed as they walked side by side.

I want to tell you three stories that will always stand out in my mind. The first one is the day we met with one of the Sinn Fein leaders. He had agreed to meet us at the monument of a young man who had been shot by British soldiers. The man's family had re-quested to meet with us, but something else had cropped up, so the Sinn Fein leader came instead. I didn't know who this man was, but it was obvious that he was important because of all the bodyguards around. Ian Bothwell came with us that day and I was pleased he did as this was his patch and he is obviously greatly respected.

After explaining what we were doing in Ireland, John asked if we could pray at this monument, it seemed such a small thing that we could do for this family. The man replied saying that he didn't pray himself, but he had no problem with us doing so. As we prayed, we asked the Lord to forgive all the violence and the killing that has taken place over the years. There have been far too many young lives lost and this young man was one of them. Many of us wept. When the prayer time had finished, the man who also had tears in his eyes, waited for a while before he spoke. "I am fed up with written prayers, today you all prayed from your hearts." He then gave us his blessing as we went on our way. Nobody knows for sure what God did that day for that man, but I know He touched him deeply.

The second story was the day we walked into Belfast. I had a vision/picture from the film *The Dam Busters*. I was reminded that in the film, the bombs are dropped and they bounce across the water before hitting the dam. The impact of each bomb caused considerable damage, but only one bomb burst the dam. I felt God say "All the prayers are like the bombs, they keep hitting the target, making it weaker, until one day it will burst, but no one will know whose prayer burst the dam, only I know." This made me think of all the people who have prayed over the years for this land. Sometimes we think that we are the only ones praying, but we are not. The prayer that finally breaks the divide could be from someone from the very estate we were passing right then, maybe a little old lady who had prayed faithfully for years. After a while, we stopped for a coffee break and I felt it was important to share this with John. He couldn't believe his ears. He told me that the night before they came to Ireland, he couldn't sleep. To pass the time he thought he would watch a film to take his mind off the walk. So he watched *The Dam Busters*. Through the film, he felt God say that the dam that was blocking His purpose here was going to burst. God always knows how to encourage His people to keep going!

The third story was on the last official day of the walk. I asked God "Is this the walk you have spoken to me about and has it fulfilled what you have called me to do? If it has, then please tell me." We walked around the city of Belfast, stopping to pray at significant sites. I remember that it was quite an emotional day. We had all got to know each other well and it's always sad when good times come to an end. However, we knew that this was only a small part of what we were feeling. You couldn't help but see the pain on the faces of the local people, they had seen hard times and I am sure most of them longed for the troubles to end.

We returned to the church and as I entered the kitchen area, a gentleman called to me to talk with him about Cromwell." I was quite surprised, as I hadn't spoken to him before. "What do you want to know?" I replied. "Just tell me what God has been saying to you about him." As I was recalling the story in bite-size pieces, I could see that he was quite overcome. "You do know that this walk hasn't done the job that God has called you to do, don't you?" He said "I have prayed for a long time for God to send someone to deal with this particular issue." This was just what I needed to hear, God was answering my prayer from earlier that day!

I could see that he wanted to say something else, so I waited. "Shirley, I have a confession to make. I do work in Tanzania and I live in Leeds, but I actually come from Dublin. I go up and down the A1 road a lot and every time I pass Huntingdon, I say 'No good thing will ever come out of that town; it's a place of death.' Now I am sitting with someone from that town who has a heart to see healing in my land. How dare I say such a thing?" He said that until then he hadn't thought about what he was saying and he was sorry for the negative words he had spoken over the town. We had a time of prayer and confession, and he asked the Lord to forgive him and set Huntingdon free. We believe that God has shown us that Huntingdon's redemptive purpose is to birth new things, good things, however people like this gentleman, whose hearts are still carrying the pain of centuries ago, still blame and even curse Huntingdon because it is Cromwell's birthplace. God wants both them and us to be free from all this negative thinking.

One evening, people started to question Stephen and I about Huntingdon. They were very touched that we had come on the walk, but even more so when they realised that Huntingdon was the birthplace of Cromwell. As we continued to talk over our meal, the idea of organising a walk like this in Huntingdonshire started to grow. Our excitement grew even more when several people from Ireland said that they would love to come and bless our town. This touched us both. We returned to Huntingdon with a feeling of excitement and expectancy. Jesus said *"Bless those who curse you"* (Luke 6 v 28). What a privilege it would be for us to have friends from Ireland come to bless our area!

Walking and Praying through Huntingdonshire wasn't just a good idea, it was a vision that God had laid on our hearts ever since John Mulinde's first visit. Many of us had prayer walked before, but never on this scale. Huntingdonshire is a rural area made up of lots of small villages and we wanted to make sure that as many as possible were included in our route.

Over the years, I have read many books about winning your town or city for God. One thing that comes over loud and clear is that God has a purpose for every place and our prayers can make a difference. So we knew that before we did anything more, we must spend time fasting and praying, seeking God's strategy. So, over the next few months, many Christians from all denominations came together to cry out to God for the brokenness in our area.

I remember one night having a dream. It was of the starting line in a marathon, but instead of runners, it had a roll of carpet tied up with string. At each end of the carpet a brilliant light shone out, and on it was written "GOD'S GLORY". The words came "My glory is ready to be rolled out before you, just cut the string." We felt God was saying that He is waiting for us to be obedient to His call and take the steps that are necessary to cut the string that is holding us back from knowing Him more fully.

Our monthly Prayer and Praise gathering carried on as usual and it was at one of these that I met Vanessa. Stephen and I were sharing our vision and the connection with Ireland and commented how many people in Huntingdonshire, and on Huntingdon Town

Council at that time, had Irish surnames. We split up into small groups to pray and I sat with Vanessa. She soon told me that she was new to the area and that her surname was Murphy. You can't get much more Irish than that! God knew what He was doing, as Vanessa was going to play an important role later on.

Chapter Eight
Walking Huntingdonshire

We were all so busy during the next few months that the start of the walk in September 2000 seemed to creep up on us. I woke early that first morning, feeling excited but also a little apprehensive. I wondered if we had done all we could and if people were going to support us. God had a few lessons to teach me over the next few days and the first came when we gathered for a commissioning service in St Mary's Church, Huntingdon.

I sat amazed as I watched about a hundred people, including clergy and civic dignitaries from all around our area, join us. It was midweek and I hadn't expected this. What little faith I had! I soon found myself in tears as everyone raised their voices in praise singing "For all the years our God has kept and guided." The unity between us was tangible and I was once again reminded of Psalm 133, "*When brothers dwell in unity ... God commands a blessing.*"

During the service, the then Bishop of Huntingdon, Rt Rev John Flack, was to commission us. I hadn't expected Stephen to ask me at the last minute to say a few words. I should have guessed that he would, as he had done this to me many times before! However, this day was different and I was a bit nervous as I walked out to the front. As I turned around and saw the sea of faces, I realised what a faithful God we serve! There was a wonderful sense of God's presence in the Church that day. The excitement grew as a large crowd, including the Bishop of Huntingdon and the Mayor of St Neots, set off down the High Street on a walk that was to take the next eleven days.

At the evening celebration, I was pleased to see the Mayor of St Neots again, this time accompanied by his deputy. After a short time of testimony, Stephen asked all the leaders, both civic and church, if they would like us to pray for them and I was pleased when they all agreed. It was an immense privilege for me, and extremely humbling. We were unaware at the time, but were told later, that until the walk, the church leaders in the town had never met each other. Afterwards, they pledged to continue to work together for God's Kingdom. This news made everything worthwhile and I know that this still continues today. Praise you Lord!

Each morning, we gathered together for prayer and to commit everything to God. We also anointed our shoes with oil before we set off. In Joshua 1 v 4, it says "*I will give you every place you set your foot*". As oil is a symbol of the Holy Spirit, it was fitting to do this as a symbolic act of God's blessing on each step we were about to take. We had decided in advance that we would sometimes need to split into smaller groups to cover a larger area. For safety's sake, we made sure that each group had some form of transport available and people ready to give refreshment and first aid when needed.

As we walked out of one town we crossed over a busy dual carriageway. I looked down from the flyover at all the cars speeding past and asked if we could stop and pray, as there had been many accidents on this road recently. Stephen agreed. As he was praying, I glanced down at his feet and saw audio tape tied around the barrier. We had two young girls with us that day and they both wondered what on earth I was doing as I started to unravel this tape. It stretched from one side of the flyover to the other, even at one point being tied to a brick and woven through the bars. I explained that people involved in the occult record curses onto tape and put it along roads and bridges and other significant places to cause disruption and accidents.

Although I knew they trusted me, they needed to know how I knew this. So, I told them of the seminar on spiritual warfare I had attended, where the man who led it had been involved in witchcraft before he became a Christian. He told us many things and this in particular, he said, was common practice. It straight away made sense to me that if we can bless people and places in the name of

Jesus, then the opposite can also happen. When the girls heard this, they too started to gather up the tape and we were amazed how much we collected. Not wanting to carry it around with us all day, we decided to burn it, to symbolically break its power and declare that the name of Jesus is more powerful. This proved to be more difficult than we thought, it didn't want to burn, but just as we have to persevere in prayer to see the enemy's strongholds fall, so it was the same for us this day.

We all enjoyed walking around the countryside, seeing all the crops being harvested and the fields prepared for next year's seed. It spoke to us of how God longs to break up the ground of our hearts to prepare us for the new seed of His word to be sown. Another aspect of the walk was that many of the places we visited had been badly affected during the Civil War. I remembered reading in local history books about how Cromwell and his men desecrated many churches for having a communion rail, as this was thought to be idolatrous. It also became common for a Priest to be imprisoned for bowing the knee in worship.

As we entered each village, we were pleased to find many of the churches open and people getting ready for Harvest Festival. I remember one place in particular. As we approached the door, we could see two ladies busily arranging flowers, so I quickly explained what we were doing. They were so touched that we had bothered to visit them that they gave us the freedom to wander around and pray wherever we liked. Before we left, they called us over and asked if we would pray with them. One of the ladies told us that they had been going through quite a hard time and felt very discouraged and that if something didn't happen soon, the church was going to die. "Please," they asked "could you pray for God to come and breathe new life into us and the church." I didn't say anything at the time, but I knew that during the Civil War, the Priest here had been put in prison, and as a result he had lost his livelihood and the community here had died.

It is always a pleasure to pray and encourage God's people, but because I knew what had happened here, it was even more special for me to be able to pray for God's Spirit to bring new life where once Cromwell's army had brought death. In our preparation, we had asked God to give us a verse of scripture for each place that we were to visit. We planned to plant this with a mustard seed as a prophetic act that as the seed grows so will the truth of God's word to them. Their faces were a picture as we shared the scripture we had been given for them, Isaiah 43 v 18-19, "*Forget the former things, do not dwell on the past. See, I am doing a new thing. Now it springs up, do you not perceive it? I am making a way in the desert and streams in the wasteland.*" We left two very happy ladies that day and who knows, perhaps soon we will hear of a revival breaking out there!

We could tell so many stories of how God met with people who were going through difficult times and how He touched them deeply. Sadly, we found that all too often people have left the church because they have been hurt. I met one such couple just before the walk. As I listened to their story, I was saddened because it was typical of so many others, but it was also obvious that they had some regrets and longed to be reconciled to their local community. It was getting near lunchtime the day we arrived in their village, so we headed straight for the church, but it wasn't open. We hadn't planned to meet this couple, so it was a lovely surprise when they turned up, followed soon after by one of the churchwardens. I thought this might cause a little embarrassment for both parties, but I was wrong. Without any hesitation, they started to tell the warden what we were doing and asked if we could look around the church.

We talked for a time and both parties had an opportunity to say what was on their hearts, and before long they both expressed a desire to deal with the old problem. It's hard to put into words how we felt that day, but we were all extremely moved, and many of us were in tears as we watched these people humble themselves before God and ask forgiveness from each other and from Him. Following this, they made a pledge that in future, they would work together for God's Kingdom in that place, so that the church's mission could be restored.

We then followed them outside to plant the word and the seed in the churchyard together, and this time, it was watered with tears of joy. In 2 Corinthians 5 v 17-20, it tells how God has given us the ministry of reconciliation, "*All this is from God, who reconciled us to himself through Christ, and gave us the ministry of reconciliation.*" We left there knowing what an awesome God we serve!

At the end of the first week, Fiona Abbot from Radio Cambridgeshire rang me. She wanted to get up-to-date news ready to go out on the radio the following day. Fiona was a great encouragement to us and her enthusiasm and excitement showed as she talked with the team. I found it very interesting as I sat back and listened to each one telling their stories. They spoke of seeing reconciliation between church groups and families, and restored visions to those who had lost hope, and how they had been encouraged by the unity as they walked with Christians from many denominations.

If one village were to stick out in my mind, it would be Warboys, as this was my home town. Once again, it had rained rather heavily all morning and we were soaked through by the time we arrived there. The Manor House, next to the church, has an annexe which the owners were more than happy for us to use to dry out. After lunch, we set off again past the Jubilee Clock, with its witch weather-vane. (Warboys is the village where Alice Samuel was accused of witchcraft and the children still wear a witch on their school badge.) As we continued down the High Street, we passed a fruit shop, where curious eyes were watching us. Stephen thought it would be a good idea to go in and explain what we were doing. They seemed genuinely interested and told us that it was a sad time for the village as a young girl who was well-liked had committed suicide. Our hearts went out to them and we said that we would pray for them and the family. We went back outside, where we stood in silence for a short time before asking for the arms of God to bring comfort, peace and love to the grieving family. We looked up and there stood the two ladies. "If more people cared like you have done, the world would be a better place!" they said and then handed us some fruit to take with us on our journey.

That evening at the celebration, we were joined by our Irish friends, including Ian from Crossfire Trust. The Trust runs a second-hand clothing project called "Worn Again". When Ian and Pauline moved in, they wanted to serve the local community in a practical way. So a shop was opened, not only to sell second-hand goods, tea, and coffee, but also to care for people's personal needs and help in any way possible. Often that's only by offering a listening ear. He told us how before he left that day, a father and son had given their lives to Jesus at the shop. He said this was the first time in ten years of working on that particular project that anyone had done this. A local pastor who was a regular visitor to Little Hey prison also told us about an inmate that week who had asked how to become a Christian. At this point God reminded me of the principle of sowing and reaping.

We had seen how division and death was sown into Ireland by Cromwell and his men and we had reaped this, with division between churches, towns, as well as families. When people think of Huntingdon, they are likely to use the words, "It's dead." I believe it is more than that, as it has had a spiritual deadness. It has been a very hard area to pray and share our faith with others. Now, here we are hearing good stories and I was being reminded of that principle again. Only this time it was different. Now we were reaping good things. I believed the blessings of this walk would go on.

On the final day, I was allocated the Huntingdon town centre group and I was very pleased when our Irish friends decided to join me. I wondered how they would feel being in "Cromwell Country". We started at the north end of the High Street, where the Cromwell Clinic is situated. This old house is built on the site of the house where Oliver Cromwell was born. I knew this would be a test for our friends, as in the past I have known Irish people who didn't want to come anywhere near our town, let alone stand on the site of his birth. Ian found it particularly hard when he saw the famous quotes about Cromwell set in the pavement. I remember him saying, "I know this is a deep area of pain, and only those who are well-healed can really participate." They didn't want to stay too long, so after a short prayer, we walked on. Next, we came to the Cromwell Museum. This building is in the centre of town and was once the Grammar School, which Samuel Pepys, as well as Oliver Cromwell, attended. Opposite the museum stands All Saints Church, where the Cromwell family vault lies. Once again, Ian found this area hard. He is a very sensitive man and cares deeply for his countrymen and their pain.

I recognise that not all Irish people feel the same about our town, it depends where you come from, and what has affected your family history. However, I began to see that as a town, we need to own the whole story of Cromwell, not just the bits that we like, because by ignoring the rest it's as though we are saying that the innocent victims did not matter, when in fact they do. We all found this day quite challenging, but it helped me to see Huntingdon through the eyes of my Irish friends.

We ended the prayer walk as we had begun with a service of celebration. How it lifted our spirits as Christians from across the county came together to raise their voices in praise and worship! That night, we heard many testimonies from the walkers, and both Ian Bothwell and our speaker, Rachel Hickson, challenged us to be community shepherds. As the evening came to an end, my tears started to flow, and the more we sang, the more I cried. Rachel came down from the stage and put her arm around me saying, "You have done a good job, Shirley. God is pleased with you. Something has been birthed here and it's a boy." There's that word "birth" again. God reminded me that Huntingdon is a place of birthing things, new things. I wasn't sure what the boy bit meant, but I was sure God would make that clear later if He needs to.

During the walk, we had such a wonderful time together and it was hard to believe it was over. But, as God said to us many times while we were on our walk, "*See, I am doing a new thing.*" (Isaiah 43 v 9a.) I remembered the vision of the roll of carpet and praised God for letting us see a glimpse of His glory in other people's lives. Without exception, we all felt it was important to continue to pray for the places where we have been. As scripture says "*He who began a good work in you will bring it to completion.*" (Philippians 1 v 6.)

Chapter Nine

A One-Legged Man

The walk had encouraged Stephen greatly, so much so that he suggested it would be a good idea to do it all again! This needed a lot of prayer, as we weren't sure this was the right direction for us to go at that time. A few days later, God started to teach me the principles of "Maintaining the victory" that we had won. He showed me that;

1) It is important to maintain the corporate prayer, as well as encourage others from different nations to pray too. This made me think of Uganda and Ireland.
2) Do not be surprised at a backlash.
3) Make sure to follow things up. Many times before an event we pray so hard. It is just as important to keep that up afterwards to maintain the ground that has been won.
4) Ask the Lord for the next step. We do not have the answers, God does.

Although I thought Stephen's idea to repeat the Huntingdonshire walk was a good one, I couldn't help but wonder when we were going to address the Irish issue. We were still meeting for prayer in Katie's office in the town centre and on one particular occasion, I had a very strange picture of a man, with only one leg. What seemed even more peculiar was that the man had only one crutch, and this was on his good side. It was quite late by now, so I asked everyone to take this away and ask God if it had any significance.

I was reading a book at this time called *Operation Exodus* by Gustav Scheller. The book tells the incredible story of his role in the return of many Jews to the Promised Land (Israel). As I was reading, it struck me there were many parallels in his story to those in mine, and how the Irish, like the Jews, had been scattered around the world. I couldn't believe what I was reading as I came to page 125, "If we do not also recognise the role of Israel as we enter the end times, we are only standing on one leg." What was God trying to say to me?

The next morning, the telephone rang. Two people saying the same thing; the good leg represented Huntingdon, and the damaged leg Ireland. They felt that if we did another walk around Huntingdon, we would only be propping up our own good side. However, we needed to address what had caused the other leg to be so badly damaged. This was the side that needed our attention. The scripture we were given was from Hebrews 12 v 13, "*Make level paths for your feet, so that the lame may not be disabled, but rather healed.*" Once again we asked God to confirm this.

A few weeks later, I met up with a very old friend, whom I hadn't seen for some time. I was telling her the story and shared the picture of the one-legged man. She looked at me and smiled "Well Shirley," she said "I am going to blow your socks off." Years ago, her mother and aunt bought a bungalow as a retreat house. She told me that a man from Northern Ireland was staying there. He had been involved in a nasty road accident and had severely damaged his leg. "It was so bad at first, that they thought they would have to amputate," she said, "however with all the prayer, thankfully that didn't happen, but unfortunately he did lose an arm." She went on. "As a result, he has to have his crutch on his good side!" Well, I couldn't believe my ears, this was exactly the picture I had seen! Without a doubt, we felt God was pointing us towards a visit to Ireland.

I am sure sometimes people think I make these stories up, but believe me I don't have that sort of imagination! Besides, God always makes sure that at least one other person can confirm everything, and on this occasion it was Katie and Annette.

I was aware that God had not yet given us a clear strategy for the reconciliation walk in Ireland. However, we felt it was important to continue to build relationships and trust with people, which in turn breaks down barriers. So, I asked God the question, "Which part of Ireland do you want me to go to this time?" I didn't have to wait long for the answer, because within days I received an invitation from Ian, to go to "Crossfire Trust" for their St Patrick's Day celebration. As I continued to read the letter, I noticed that the finale to their events was to be a dinner in a marquee. This really made me think. You see God had been talking to me about His tent of meeting, the place where His glory is found. We took this as a good indication that the time was right to return to Ireland.

However, after all God had done over the years, I still had my doubts about myself. Why me, Lord? What had I got to give? I didn't even feel I had any particular gift. I'm not a theologian or historian, I'm not even particularly clever. Yes, I care for others and I do have a heart for my town and for the places like Ireland, which Huntingdon has affected in the past through Cromwell. I had just got to trust God.

That week I joined the prayer cell for Huntingdon. I told them about my forthcoming trip to Ireland and asked if they would pray for me, but I didn't tell them how inadequate I was feeling. God is so faithful! He gave someone a picture of me being handed loaves and fishes, and she told me, "Jesus says remember what I did with the loaves and fishes!" This was a great reminder to me that, just like the young boy in the Bible had given his lunch, all I had to do was give what I had and let God do the rest. Another had a picture of a map of the British Isles and I was lying like a bridge between England and Ireland, and he had the song "Bridge over troubled waters, I will lay me down." I felt a little uncomfortable as only Jesus can bridge the gap, but as His representative God wanted me to hear this and you will see why later in the story.

The more I thought about this calling, the more overwhelmed I felt. There was so much to do and I didn't have a clue where to start. I didn't realise it until then that God has such a sense of humour! As I recalled some of the things God had promised, I remembered the text that He first gave to me back in 1990, Joshua chapter 1 v 3. "*I will give you every place you set your foot.*" Lord, I understand what you are saying but this is a huge thing, it seems too big a task for me. It was then that I felt Him say "Why do you think I gave you big feet?" I have always hated the fact that I have such large feet, for I take a size 9. I shared this with Vanessa and Annette that evening and we just fell about laughing!

Before going to Ireland this time, I felt it was important to go and see Father Nicholas Kearney, our local Catholic Priest. Although Stephen had always kept the ministers informed, I wanted to bring everything into the open and I didn't want to do anything that could be misunderstood. I talked to Stephen and he arranged a visit later that week. I didn't know Father Nicholas very well and I am sure he didn't fully understand why I needed to see him. However, I knew it was right, especially because of the many people with Irish roots in his church. I have great respect for this man and even though he didn't fully grasp everything I had said, he blessed me anyway, and then asked if on my return I would go and share with his congregation. I left his home that day with a feeling of peace and excitement and I wondered what God had in store for me.

March is a lovely time of the year to be travelling to Ireland and I was looking forward to seeing my friends again. Unfortunately, the outbreak of foot and mouth was something I hadn't thought about and how it was to affect my time there. The disease spreads very rapidly and because in Ireland they rely heavily on their livestock, they couldn't afford to take any risks. So, as a precaution any unnecessary events were cancelled, including those at Crossfire.

The cancellations meant Ian had some spare time and he offered to take me down to Drogheda. As this was one of the places I really wanted to go, I couldn't resist the opportunity. I remember the day well, because as we walked around the town and towards St Lawrence's Gate, I couldn't help but think how strange it felt, as if I shouldn't be there. Was this, I wondered, because I knew the history, and how many had died trying to resist Cromwell's attack? I don't know, but I knew that I would be back one day.

St Patrick's Day arrived and it was decided that we would all go and visit Downpatrick Cathedral, the place where Patrick is thought to be buried. We wanted to celebrate the life of this godly man so we gathered around his grave for a short time of worship and prayer. When we had finished, we turned around and looked out over Ireland and prayed "Please God, would you birth again the spirit that was in Patrick, please birth it again Lord." We repeated this over and over again. Little did I know it then, but back home things were happening that once again would blow my mind.

At the airport, I telephoned Tony to let him know I was on my way. "Have you seen the news?" were almost his first words. "No" I replied "I have been a bit cut off from all of that." He continued, "It's nothing bad, but you need to go and buy a newspaper and be prepared for a shock." I promptly did, and inside was a picture of our very dear friends and prayer partners, Beryl and Lance Ayres, with a baby that had been abandoned on their doorstep!

On the night of St Patrick's Day, they went to bed as usual. They hadn't been in bed long when Lance heard a strange noise outside. He got up and opened the front door. He couldn't see anything straight away, but then he heard the noise again. Looking down, he noticed a bundle lying on the ground. It was a newborn baby boy, wrapped in a cloth. Lance was soon joined by Beryl, they couldn't believe it, they were both in shock. (Mind you, if the little chap was to be left anywhere, I couldn't think of a better place and I'm sure the mother thought so too.) They quickly called the police and ambulance service and the baby was taken to hospital where he was given the name Patrick!

Who would believe that you could pray a prayer in Ireland about birthing again the spirit of Patrick, and a baby be left on your prayer partners' doorstep that very night who was then given the name Patrick? God had been saying to us for some time how our area was closely connected to Ireland, and what affects one will affect another. The Biblical principle of what you sow, you shall reap, but I didn't think that meant literally!

On my return, I felt very privileged to speak in the Catholic Church. I was amazed when Father Nicholas telephoned me to say that I was to be given time in all three services that weekend. I have always respected the feelings of the Catholic people about the Cromwell issue, and I didn't want to open old wounds. However, this is about God's healing plan for the Irish people in Huntingdon as well as in Ireland.

I made it clear as I was talking, that I have never been pro- or anti-Cromwell. It is all about God wanting to heal the wounds of injustice in history and the role He has given me in that. I was honest and said that I didn't know where this was going to lead, but I knew that God was guiding me along the way. It was a time that I will always treasure, not only for the opportunity to tell the story, but for the unity I felt as I shared this time with them.

We had always known that to encourage unity amongst Christians and to seek reconciliation where necessary was on God's heart. Whether that was between us, or between brothers and sisters across the sea in Ireland, it makes no difference, we are to break down the barriers that divide. Although I have no doubt in my mind of the need to heal past wounds, I know that others disagree. All I can say is that the healing many of us have received as individuals, I believe God longs to do for our churches and communities, to set them free too.

Because I am no theologian, I asked God for a scripture in the New Testament that would confirm that the sins of the past affect the present. I had long been aware of 1 Peter 1 v 13-23, "*Be Holy*", and in particular, v 18, *"For you know that it was not with perishable things that you were redeemed from the empty way of life handed down to you from your forefathers, but with the precious blood of Christ.."* However, this time I was looking for words from Jesus himself. I was led to Luke 11 v 50-51. Jesus was talking to the religious leaders about how they were treating both Him and the prophets; *"Therefore, this generation will be held responsible for the blood of all the prophets that has been shed since the beginning of the world, ... Yes I tell you, this generation will be held responsible for it all."* They had failed to see their own sin. They looked good on the outside, but inside they were still full of sin and hypocrisy. They said they wouldn't have killed the prophets of old, but Jesus knew they would have done, because they were sadly too full of their own importance. Right through history, God's prophets had been rejected and now they were rejecting God Himself in Jesus, the greatest prophet of all. Past sins of others had caught up with them.

We hear people say "Oh, that's in the past." And so it is, until something comes up that is connected in some way and up it jumps to remind you of what happened, and the pain and the anger continues. It may be under the surface, but it's still in the memory of the place, and therefore it will affect your worship and relationship with God and each other. 1 Corinthians chapter 4 v 5b, *"He* (God the Holy Spirit) *will bring to light what is hidden in darkness."* As Jesus is the light of the world, therefore as you bring those things into His light, the darkness has no hold anymore, Satan has to let go and the pain is healed. I am not saying that we have to spend all our time looking backwards, and trying to find reasons for our sin. We have to say as David in Psalm 139 said, *"See if there is any offensive way in me and lead me in the way everlasting."*

So let me ask you a question. Are there things in your family line that are preventing you or your loved ones from knowing the fullness of God's blessing? It may be something like freemasonry. Oaths made by masons block the flow of God the Holy Spirit in your life and your family's life and even the life of your church. Or it could be adultery, atheism, or something that seems simple, such as broken relationships. Perhaps you have said or done something for which you need to say sorry. Don't hold back. If possible go and see the people involved. I promise you, it's worth it!

Are you or your family into reading horoscopes or playing with ouija boards? Harmless fun people may say, but it isn't. In Deuteronomy 18 v 9-13, it tells you that "*these practices are detestable to the Lord*" and it starts you on the road to idolatry and the occult, which not only invites God's enemy into your life, but it also involves putting your trust in something other than God. Jesus came to set you free from all this.

Perhaps you're that someone who has been hurt by a church leader or another member. Do you find it hard to forgive? Maybe this has led you to turn your back not only on the church but on God too. I don't know, but what I do know is that if you ask God to help, He will show you the way and help you to forgive. He might start with something in your own life that needs His divine touch, but that's because He loves you and longs to restore your life. Then as you allow Him in to transform you, this will draw you closer to Him, which will then open the way for you to pray more effectively for your family, church and area and maybe even your nation.

Now what about Shirley, you may ask? Well, God is still working on me too. Even as I write this, God has been showing me areas of my life that need His help. Over the years, He has shown me that because of the low opinion I had of myself, I had spent almost my entire life worrying what other people thought about me. As I repented and received His forgiveness, I grew in faith and trust and learned to let go. It really doesn't matter what people think, what matters most is that God loves us unconditionally. Many times, over the years I have been tempted to give up when the road seemed too rough. Just like everyone else, I struggle in prayer and sometimes lose my way, but God, in His faithfulness and love, brings me back.

In the Spring of 2001, a few of us attended Spring Harvest, a Christian festival held every Easter. On the last day, we met up with a group from my church. I didn't think anything of it at the time, but later on our way home, one of the ladies said, "Shirley, when you greeted us this morning you gave us a beautiful smile. At that moment, I saw you change into a beautiful young radiant bride."

She continued, "I feel God is saying to you it is time for change." Within a short while of her saying this, a new name for our group popped into my head, "Arise Ministries." Later, as I shared this with Annette, she said, "Do you realise what has happened? You have been given a new name, just as brides get a new name on their wedding day!"

Walking and Praying through Huntingdonshire was a bit too long. We had known it would have to change. However again, my fear of people came into play. "What will they think? What if they think I am getting a bit above myself?" I had been hurt many times by other people's comments and accusations. I knew I would have to wait for God's leading on this, and be obedient to Him. I didn't have to wait too long, because soon after this Stephen, with whom I hadn't shared my thoughts, preached on how, when God calls you, He gives you a new name. He shared the examples of Abram to Abraham, Sarai to Sarah, Jacob to Israel, and Saul to Paul to name a few. So *Arise Ministries* was birthed!

Around this time, I had been challenged as I read Mahesh Chavda's book, *The Hidden Power of Prayer and Fasting.* Reading the wonderful stories of God's mercy and healing really inspired me. Fasting has been a practice of mine for many years, especially at times of big changes or missions. However, this time I felt God was calling me to take it more seriously than I had in the past. So I decided to have three days of fasting and seeking God's will.

On the third day, I was reading the Bible from the book of Ezekiel chapter 37. I had read the story of the valley of dry bones before, but on this occasion, I went on to the next few verses, under the heading in my Bible of "One Nation under One King". It tells the story of God speaking to Ezekiel about His divided people. God told him to take a stick and write on it, "*Belonging to Judah and the Israelites associated with him.*" Then God told him to take another stick and write on it, "*Ephraim's stick, belonging to Joseph and all the house of Israel associated with him.*" One was the northern kingdom and the other was the southern kingdom. As I was reading, I could again see clearly the parallels between Israel and Ireland. Both of them are divided into North and South, and just like the Israelites, Irish people have been scattered around the world.

As I read on, I felt that God was revealing to me how the similarities between them were not just a coincidence. It was as if I was reading about Ireland and His love for the Irish people, and how one day, the world will see what He, the Sovereign Lord had done for them. This scripture was as relevant to them today as it was to Israel long ago. I could feel the presence of God as I prayed more about this. I could have stayed there all day, but I had to get on. However, one thing I knew for sure was the importance of taking this thought and testing it that night when I met up for prayer with Annette and Vanessa.

By the time I arrived at Vanessa's house, I was quite excited. I couldn't wait to share what I had been feeling and as we read Ezekiel together the presence of God came flooding into the room just the same as earlier. The three of us just sat quiet for a while. We felt that God had given us a revelation of His heart for the Irish people, but what now God? I opened my eyes and looked up. We were all kneeling on the floor and I noticed that Annette was looking rather low, as if she was carrying a heavy burden. Then, and I didn't at the time know why, but I took Vanessa's hand and laid it on Annette's. Immediately the two hands touched, Vanessa broke down in tears. Not just a few, she was sobbing, face down on the carpet.

It suddenly occurred to me that Annette is married to a Protestant from Northern Ireland, Vanessa is married to Derek, whose family was Catholic and originally from the Republic of Ireland (sometimes called the South), and I am married to Tony, a man born and bred in Huntingdon, Cromwell's home town. This I could see was a picture of the unity that God wants His people to have. No one spoke for a while. However, I knew God was saying that His plan was to bring the two sides together, but their pain was in the way. I also had to accept that what Cromwell had done played a big part of this pain. As we left that night, I asked both of them to bring a stick from their gardens to the core group meeting the following evening.

I was shocked when I saw Annette arriving with a two-foot long stick! "Oh no," I thought, "How am I going to explain this to the others?" I honestly thought the stick would be shorter, and therefore give me time to share. Oh well, I thought, I shall just have to fill them in straight away. So I asked Vanessa if she had brought her stick. She bent down and pulled it out from under the chair. I couldn't believe my eyes, for it was exactly the same length as Annette's! Everyone in the room laughed, but not one of them had any idea what this was about.

As I held the two sticks in my hand, I told them all about the previous day. Then I asked them "What can you see?" Immediately someone said that they were both the same length. "That's right," I said "Both are equal in God's sight, but what else can you see?" They all had to agree that one was green, smooth and quite healthy looking, whilst the other one was dry, gnarled and broken. "The healthy one," I said "is from Vanessa's garden and it represents the Republic (Southern Ireland), but the broken one is from Annette's garden and this represents Northern Ireland (the North). Tonight we are going to do some prophetic intercession and use this scripture in Ezekiel to pray for Ireland."

I wrote "North" on Annette's stick and "South" on Vanessa's, and bound them together with tape. Then, as I held them in my hand, we prophetically prayed that as the wounds in Ireland were healed, people would be able to forgive and turn again to God, and be one nation under one King, Jesus.

Chapter Ten

Nehemiah Points the Way

Time marched on and in 2001 Katie and other members of the team, moved away. I was feeling vulnerable, especially as Stephen too was moving on. Up to this point, I had been so sure that God wanted us to go to Ireland and address the Cromwell issue, but now with Stephen going, I started to have some doubts.

I was at this time reading about the Jews rebuilding Jerusalem in Ezra chapter 4. In verse 21 it tells how King Artaxerxes called a halt to the building for a time because of his fear of another revolt. In my Bible footnotes it said, "Setbacks and standstills are painful, yet circumstances sometimes really are beyond our control. When you have been brought to a standstill, remember to still stand strong in the Lord." I felt that this was God's word for me. As I was so unsure of the way forward, I believe He was telling us to stop for a while and listen to Him.

This became a very special time for us as we allowed God to speak into this situation. Months of waiting had passed, when one day I received a telephone call from Janet, our prayer partner in Dublin. She told me that when she first came to Huntingdonshire, she felt as though there was a large cloud over the area. It was so heavy that she had to go elsewhere to pray. At that moment, God reminded me of what He had told us many times about the Civil War and in particular, Cromwell's part in it. It was like a thick cloud over us and until the pain and wrongs were addressed, this cloud would not go away.

In the days that followed, I continued to study Ezra. I felt God's encouragement to me to "Get back to what I have called you to do, stop looking at yourself, look to me." One thing the enemy loves to do is to tempt us to take our eyes off God and focus on our problems. I was so busy looking and worrying about the changes that were taking place around me, that I had taken my eyes off Him and the calling on my life. God told me quite firmly that I was to stick to the task and that as we prayed and fasted, He would give us His direction. He continued by saying that following Him was going to be costly in many ways, financially, in time and personally. This was a challenge not only to me, but to the entire team.

How did I feel at this time? Well, if I am honest, it was both scary and awesome. So let me remind anyone reading this if you are having doubts about your calling, or feel discouraged, then just turn back to God. Listen again to the promises in His word. Don't be afraid if you have got things wrong. God is bigger than our mistakes and He will guide you back, if that is your heart's desire. Also, look again at the promises He has made to you personally. We have a covenant-keeping God. People will let us down, but He never will. He keeps all His promises. So take heart, we have all been there. It isn't always easy, but then Jesus never said it would be.

After the walk around Huntingdonshire, many people were challenged about where they attended church. Annette was one of those. She felt that as her heart was to pray for the people where she lived, it wasn't right to worship four or so miles away. Then, a while later, Tony and I were also challenged about returning to worship in our own town. I found this amazing because once upon a time, I really hated Huntingdon and tried so hard to move away, far away. However, God kept me here and over the years as He changed me and my perspective of the town. I hadn't noticed how much until now, when I realised God had given me a love for the place and the people that I know could only have come from Him.

We knew that God had allowed us the time at Hemingford Grey Church, not only to grow our faith and heal us, but also to reveal more of His purposes. After all, if we hadn't been there, we might never have met John Mulinde and this story might never have been written. Now it was time to return to our church in Huntingdon. I felt it was important before we moved to go and talk to the minister about Arise Ministries and the work that I was involved in. As I have said before, it is always important to come under the authority of your church leader. He or she is your spiritual cover and therefore needs to know what you are doing.

It had been a while since I'd had the picture of the one-legged man. At the time, we really felt that God was pointing us towards the reconciliation work in Ireland, but nothing had happened since. We had waited many years for this and God had always been faithful and shown us the way. Even so, it was hard to be patient.

One day, Stephen rang me saying that he was going to a prayer summit in Westminster, London, and wondered if I wanted to go too. As nothing else seemed to be happening, Annette and I jumped at the chance. "It's time to cross the Jordon" was one of the first sessions we heard. This reminded me of the prophecy back in 1990. *"You are to lead the people of God over the Jordan and into the land of His promise. The Jordan of today will be for you a significant crossing point of no return."* The following day, Cindy Jacobs was encouraging us to look and take more seriously the state of our land. Some of the words she used still stick in my mind. "There is civil war on our streets, young men killing young men, blood crying out for blood." Why did she use those words? I don't know, but this I did know, I felt the call to go back to Ireland very strong.

At lunchtime, Stephen introduced us to Rev Edward Wright, an Anglican Priest from Kent. Edward is a direct descendant of one of Cromwell's men who had fought alongside him in Ireland and it was his longing some day to go and seek forgiveness and reconciliation from the Irish people. This gets more and more amazing I thought! Earlier, we had heard about civil war on our streets, and here I was with someone whose ancestor was involved in that period of Irish history when so much blood was shed.

Stephen and Edward asked if we would like to go and pray outside the Houses of Parliament, where Cromwell's statue is situated. I had never been to the Houses of Parliament, nor seen the statue before. I was quite shocked when I did see it, for it was exactly what

Oliver Cromwell fought against. He hated any form of idolatry and would not have approved of this statue at all.

Many conferences that year were saying the same thing:
1) It's time to acknowledge how serious the situation is in our nation.
2) We need to pray for the church to wake up.
3) We needed to confess the sins of our area and nation.
4) We were encouraged to pray Habakkuk's prayer, "*In wrath (Lord) remember mercy.*" These teachings convinced me that we should be planning the reconciliation trip to Ireland to address the Cromwell issue. However, the most important thing was to seek God for His clear direction and strategy.

We called a time of prayer and fasting and it was during this time that I felt God talk to me through Nehemiah's prayer. I love reading this account in Chapter 1, where it tells us of Nehemiah's distress at the state of Jerusalem, the Jews' holy city. The walls had been broken down and he knew that the temple and the people were vulnerable to attack. After a time of weeping and fasting, Nehemiah recognised the need to come before a Holy God and repent of the sins of his, and his father's house. He could see clearly the Israelites' wickedness and disobedience of God's commands. He longed to return to Jerusalem, but as he was cupbearer to the Persian King, he needed the King's permission before he could go. So he asked God to give him favour in the King's presence.

In the days that followed, I continued to read Nehemiah's account and things began to get clearer. As the trip to Ireland was also about seeking to rebuild broken walls, the principles were the same as Nehemiah's. In Chapter 2 v 4, the King asks Nehemiah, "What is it you want?" and before he answered, Nehemiah prayed. Through reading Nehemiah, God showed me that:
1) Prayer has to be a priority. *Before he spoke he was afraid* (v2). God is greater than our fear, once you bring Him into the situation.

2) In verse 3, it teaches us not to be afraid to ask the right people. Nehemiah went straight to the top man, the King. This made me think about who I would need to speak to.

3) Then (v5) Nehemiah answers "*If it pleases the king and if your servant has found favour in his sight, let him send me to the city in Judah.*" This spoke to me of making sure you have the right authority.

4) In verse 6, the King asks how long? So Nehemiah set a time.

5) Nehemiah, in verse 7, made sure he had protection from surrounding countries, by asking for letters of authority and safety.

6) Nehemiah knew God's hand was upon him (v18). Knowing God is behind your task is the best incentive to move. Remember too that He doesn't only use you, He also puts other people in place.

7) There was opposition to his task (v10). Rebuilding the walls of Jerusalem was a threat to the Samaritan officials and their authority. The enemy will not like you. So be aware.

8) In verses 11-16, it talks of Nehemiah surveying the walls by moonlight to avoid unhealthy gossip. This prevented his enemies knowing what he was up to. Check your information and make sure it's accurate, but keep the plans close to your heart.

9) Nehemiah had a vision and knew there was a right time for sharing (v17). Sometimes we underestimate others, thinking they won't understand. When the time is right, share it, and then allow the Holy Spirit the freedom to impress it on them if it is right to do so.

10) Always make sure you give God the glory, (v20).

Chapter 4 goes on to tell us of the opposition to the work. Why are we always so surprised when things start to go wrong? The enemy does not want God to be glorified, so he will try anything. In Nehemiah's case, it was spotted quickly and they warned each other of danger by sounding the trumpet. That way they could carry on building the wall whilst protecting each other's backs. And so it should be for us.

We should always make sure that prayer and intercession are going on at the same time as the work.

In Chapter 5, Nehemiah's character was under attack. In verse 10, it tells how his enemies tried to get him to go into the temple, knowing that only the priests are permitted to enter. If he had given in to this temptation, it would have been a great sin, and he would have lost his credibility. When you are doing God's work, don't be afraid, but be prepared for an attack on your own character.

It was August and Stephen's departure was close. I hadn't shared any of my thoughts with him as he had enough on his plate with his move. You can imagine my delight when one Sunday morning, he preached on Nehemiah and the building and protecting of the wall! I cried as I listened, for I felt God was saying "You're on track Shirley, you're on track". Although I wasn't looking forward to Stephen leaving, I knew that all would be well and God was in control. The core group was, and always has been, very supportive, and although they too wished Stephen was staying, they knew that this was part of God's plan. It was time now to move on.

September was upon us and with Stephen gone, and Tony and I back in our home church in Huntingdon, we started to concentrate on what God had being saying to us. The vision had never changed. We had always known that we would be retracing Cromwell's steps around Ireland. I felt that it was important to do this in the opposite spirit. This meant waiting outside each town to be invited in, instead of forcing ourselves onto the people and taking over. Thinking back to Nehemiah, what was God saying to us at this point? We needed to;

1) Be sure of what our task was (v4).
2) Make sure we have the authority (v5).
3) Set a time (v6).
4) Obtain letters of protection (v7).
5) Be aware of the opposition (v9-10).
6) And always give God the glory (v18, 20).

And all of this was covered with prayer, prayer and yet more prayer!

In the weeks that followed, God continued to speak to us. One evening, as we met for prayer, Vanessa had a picture of a ball of fire, with flames coming out of the top and running down the sides like veins. I was reminded of two separate things. One was way back, when I first felt God say that the root of the Civil War was like a cancer running through the veins of the country and over into Ireland. The second was Rubens' prayer back in 1999, when he saw a ball of fire being placed in my hands which, he said, was for the healing of the nations. I didn't understand fully what this meant, but I knew the Irish people had been scattered around the globe. So, as God healed this part of history it could affect many other nations too.

It was only a few days later that the dreadful events of September 11th 2001 occurred in New York. Our daughter, Alison, was visiting us that afternoon with her new baby, Adele. I was outside with Tony at the time when I heard Alison shout out. My stomach turned over, I thought something had happened to the baby. She called out, "A plane has just crashed into one of the Twin Towers in New York." We rushed inside, not being able to believe what we were seeing as a second plane hit the other tower. Like everyone, we will never forget that awful day as we watched helplessly the pictures unfolding on our televisions. The horror of it all is forever etched on our memories. What made the whole thing even more unbelievable was to hear later that this had been a deliberate act by Al Qu'aida. The hijackers believed that they were doing the will of God. How could anyone believe that? Then I remembered that's what Cromwell thought too.

Christmas and New Year passed and before we knew it we were in 2002. We all felt this was to be a significant year for Arise Ministries, even though we had no idea then where it would lead us. In Judah at the time of Nehemiah, there were about 50,000 Jews but strangely, there seemed very little concern among the people and officials about the state of their city walls. However, God gave the burden to Nehemiah. It was up to him to put things in place ready to rebuild and then make it happen. Although we didn't know yet what our next step was going to be, we did know we were definitely going to Ireland. So once again we started to look at what we had learned from Nehemiah. When Nehemiah received the message about the city walls, he wept and spent days fasting and praying. He went before God and poured out his heart, not just for what he needed, but more importantly, in repentance for the sins of the Israelites, including his and his father's house. We too spent time fasting and praying. I knew that God had called me to seek forgiveness for the innocent bloodshed during the Civil War. I had to be prepared to confess this not only to God, but also to the people of Ireland. Repentance opened the way for Nehemiah, just as it does for each one of us. So I must do whatever the Lord requires of me.

Secondly, I knew that like Nehemiah, I needed to know exactly what I was asking before going to see leaders from the churches and the Town Council. This led us onto the third thing and that was to set a date. Although we had a strong feeling that this was the year, we didn't know for sure, or what time of year it should be. We continued to ask God to make this clear.

Fourthly, just as Nehemiah needed letters for safe travel, we also felt we needed to take letters with us from our churches and hopefully our town leaders.

Once again, God didn't waste any time in getting the message through to us. Phyllis, our prayer partner in Omagh, Northern Ireland, sent me a copy of a book by Helen Litton, called *Oliver Cromwell: an illustrated history*. She had found this book very helpful and thought it would help us too. God was about to answer one of our prayers. I had read many books like this before, so I was aware of some of the history, such as Drogheda being the first town Cromwell had conquered in 1649. However, it wasn't until I was reading this particular book, at this particular time, that the date hit me. Drogheda was taken on September 11th. This date was so significant following the Twin Towers attack in America the previous year. I knew God was saying to me that we had to go back to Drogheda on this date.

So the next question was, which year? Again God didn't leave us wondering long. A few days later, I remembered that this was the year our Queen was celebrating her Golden Jubilee, fifty years as Monarch of our land. The Bible tells us in Leviticus 25 that the Year of Jubilee was celebrated every fifty years as a time of restoration and it included cancelling all debt, freeing all slaves, and returning all land to its original owner. I remembered how Cromwell's army drove the Catholic people off their land and over to the west of Ireland. Many died in the process or were sold as slaves to the West Indies. After the war had finished, Parliament had run out of money, so Cromwell ordered that the land and estates be distributed amongst his men as payment for their services. No wonder some Irish people still hate the English! I could see why they fight so hard to keep hold of their land, they're not going to let anyone take it from them again. I don't agree with any violence, but I could see how the memory of this time, and the innocent blood that had been shed, still affected them and their land.

God didn't leave me waiting long before He confirmed all of this to me. In the February, my "Everyday with Jesus" Bible reading notes were headed "Giving back the land, what does God mean by Jubilee Year?" I felt a burning in my spirit as I read this. I wanted so much to say sorry to the Irish people for the robbery they had endured. I had no idea how I was going to do it, but I wanted to do something and knowing this was the Queen's Jubilee year, this must be the year.

So we knew the start date for the reconciliation journey September 11th, and the year 2002, so what came next in Nehemiah? Having the right authority! As I thought about this, I felt that we couldn't approach our own leaders until we knew for sure how the people in Ireland felt about our plans. It wouldn't be right to force an apology upon them, just because we wanted to make it. It was also possible that because of our connection with Cromwell, they may not even want us to walk their land. So we decided to go to Ireland and "test the water" by calling at each town and listen to what the people there had to say, before asking their permission. Time was moving on quickly and we realised that if we were to get everything in place for the coming September, we needed to make this first trip soon.

Every weekend, Katie would telephone me from Devon, and I remember her delight when I told her of my intention to go to Ireland. "Shirley, I really feel I have to come too," she said. I was thrilled. There was no doubt that her coming on the trip made good sense because it was her grandfather, Joseph Carr, who had been Town Clerk of Drogheda. As Drogheda had been the first town to fall, it felt right that this should be our starting point. Perhaps Katie's connection with the town would open a few doors. We decided to write to the Town Clerk, to tell him of our intended visit and ask if he would see us. Katie was happy to do this and it wasn't long before she got a reply and a meeting was set up. Although the prospect of travelling to places and meeting people we didn't know was a bit daunting, God showed us once again that we had to trust Him, because He had it all in hand.

A few days later, Phyllis telephoned. I told her all the news of our proposed trip and before I had finished, she expressed a desire to join us if we would let her. Let her? I could have crawled down the phone and hugged her! I was more than happy to have her along. She had knowledge of the land and contacts with people that we didn't have, contacts that were later to prove to be invaluable.

Chapter Eleven
Testing the Vision

At the beginning of March 2002, Katie and I flew into Belfast airport. Phyllis met us with the welcome news that her husband had given us permission to use his car for the whole time that we were in Ireland. This was such a relief because before we left we had no idea how we were to get from place to place. Once again, God was faithful.

We had booked a weekend conference at The Christian Renewal Centre in Rostrevor, County Down. We thought this would be a perfect way to recharge our batteries before the journey. Little did we know that God had His own plans! Ireland is such a beautiful place and from the window of our room, we had the most breathtaking view across the bay. I hadn't realised until Phyllis told me that on the other side of the water was the Republic of Ireland. In the past this had been an area of concern, for along the coast British soldiers had been attacked and killed. As the sun set that evening, I couldn't help but wonder what it would be like when peace comes, real peace I mean.

The next morning, folk began to arrive from all over Ireland. People came from all walks of life, both Catholic and Protestant. They were just happy to be together. I continued to struggle with my shyness and meeting new people was still a bit of a problem. Having Phyllis and Katie with me helped, as they would often break the ice. Saturday afternoon was one such occasion. I was sitting having tea when I was joined by a young man who introduced himself as Stephen Forbes. Stephen came from Wexford, another town that had suffered during Cromwell's invasion. He asked me where I was from. "Huntingdon" I answered. Phyllis then added that this was the birthplace of Cromwell. "Really," he said in a surprised voice, "what has brought you here then?" I hesitated. He went on, "Have you come just for the conference?" "No" I replied and started to share with him the vision for retracing Cromwell's steps. His face just lit up. "Shirley," he said, "you have got to meet my wife, she's a Catholic. Let me go and fetch her" and he jumped up and dashed off.

In a very short time he arrived back with his wife, Georgina. As we introduced ourselves, I could see that this was a very special moment for her. As I shared a small part of my story, her eyes filled up with tears. "Oh dear," she said "oh dear me, I am absolutely speechless. I have prayed about this for so long, fancy the Lord sending you from Huntingdon." She reached across the table and took hold of my hand. As our two hands touched she started to sob.

We all knew that this was a God connection and after the weekend ended, Stephen and Georgina went back to Wexford on cloud nine, both very excited and desperate to get involved. As a Catholic, Georgina felt it was important for us to meet the Roman Catholic leaders in their town, so she said that she would try and arrange this for us. God didn't stop there either, but continued to surprise us.

On Sunday, Katie and I had joined a table of five for lunch and as we sat chatting, we realised that every one of us sat at the table was English. This seemed strange as we had really wanted to meet as many Irish people as possible. However, once again, God had His hand on it. To our amazement, one lady told us that she was a descendant of Cromwell. "But," she said "I have no knowledge of his activities in Ireland." We realised that in Britain we have been guilty of distorting history by teaching a one-sided view of what had happened. Once again, I was reminded that it's time for us to own both the good and the bad of the Civil War. If not, every time we put Cromwell on a pedestal, we not only go against his beliefs on idolatry, but we condone his actions and the pain he caused others.

After lunch, we met with Harry Smith, then the Director of the Centre. His response as I shared the vision was very encouraging. He felt that this walk would play a part in the healing process of

Ireland. Before we left, he made some suggestions as to whom we should contact, such as Augustine Reay (Gussy) from the Catholic Charismatic group in Drogheda. Thank you God, this was just what we needed names and contacts. Only God knew the people that He had prepared in advance and so, after a time of prayer and blessing, we set off feeling uplifted and ready for the task ahead.

Our first meeting the following day was at the Council Offices with Des Foley, the Town Clerk and Sean Collins from the Old Drogheda Society (Sean was also previously Mayor of the town). Des had invited Sean as he knew a lot about Katie's grandfather, as well as the Cromwell period. The meeting went better than I had anticipated. Sean was full of admiration for Joseph Carr and told us of all the good he had done for the town. I was so thankful that Katie had been able to come and hear this tribute to her grandfather. Sean went on to explain how history had distorted the facts about Cromwell's exploits. We were very much aware of this and how it depends on which side is telling the story as to how it's remembered. However, one innocent life lost is one life too many. I started to explain our plan to retrace Cromwell's steps. I pointed out the significance of the 11th September, as the date in 1649 he took the town and the terrorist attack of 2001 in America. We shared how we felt it was important for the Town Council and the churches to invite us into their town, as the opposite had happened in 1649. The idea was met with enthusiasm from both men and they suggested that we contact Huntingdon Town Council to ask if it was possible for a representative to come too. This was already on our minds, but it was good to have it confirmed. The meeting lasted about two hours and although in the end things didn't turn out quite the way we thought, we had felt welcome and knew that what God had started, He would finish.

Our second meeting was with Gussy and his friend from the Solid Rock Church. It was obvious straight away that these two got on really well and their friendly greeting made us feel as though we had known them for years. As this was their lunch break, I wondered how much I should share because I didn't feel comfortable taking up all their time. I needn't have worried though, as they told us of their passion to see men from all denominations meeting regularly for prayer. The time soon went and although they both were due back at work, they were so fired up and excited, that they didn't want to leave before we had a chance to pray together and exchange addresses. Although Gussy would be away in September, he made us a promise that he would do all he could to bring things together for our visit. Our time in Drogheda had been good.

We arrived in Dublin for a meeting that evening. We were deeply touched when they began with an Irish welcome in Gaelic. They said, "We want you to know that you are very welcome in our town." This had a strange effect on me, firstly I felt a real sense of love and unity, but I also had a deep sense of guilt and shame. Perhaps, this was because I knew their history. However, I was soon sharing my story once again. The excitement in the room was tangible. One lady said, "The people here in Ireland desperately need to hear this." Once again we were told that even now when the name of Cromwell is mentioned, it causes great pain, hurt and bitterness, and people even use his name to curse their children. I felt so ashamed and sad. Dear Lord, what have we done to these people?

We were very encouraged that evening and God confirmed so much to us of what He had said before we left England. We were again given the scripture Isaiah 62, verse 10; "*Pass through, pass through the gates! Prepare the way for the people. Build up, build up the highway! Remove the stones. Raise a banner for the nations.*" We knew God alone could remove the stones of pain that block His blessing. We just needed to follow where He leads and the prompting of the Holy Spirit. We left feeling very uplifted.

The following day, we met Paddy Monaghan. Paddy is co-editor of the book *Adventures in reconciliation; twenty-nine Catholic testimonies.* I wasn't sure what Paddy would think of our idea or even if he would be interested. This made me feel vulnerable as we approached his office. As we entered, he stood up and shook my hand and instantly put me at my ease. After telling him our plans, we waited for his response. He answered by saying that he knew without doubt that this issue was on God's heart and that it needed healing. I turned to Katie and asked her to pass me the long plastic bag. He looked puzzled as I took it from her and opened it up. Inside were the two bound sticks, representing North and South. I told him the story of how God had spoken to me through Ezekiel 37. He didn't make a comment and I wondered at first what he was thinking. Then he leaned forward and gently took the sticks from my hand and prayed the most amazing prayer that brought tears to our eyes. Paddy told us that we could use his name by way of introduction and he telephoned friends in Waterford and Cork asking if they could help us too. We came away from Dublin feeling very blessed, humbled and excited.

We had a pleasant journey down to Wexford. The countryside was beautiful and even though it was early in the year, the trees and shrubs were covered with blossom. We arrived at the guest house late in the afternoon and were shown to our lovely rooms, which were beyond our expectation. At first, I panicked, as I wondered how much this was going to cost us. Then came the biggest blessing we could have received at that time, the landlady told us that the bill had already been paid! Thank you Lord, you certainly are a God who provides!

Later on as we made our way to the evening venue, we passed the Catholic Church as well as the Friary and I wondered what stories these two buildings could tell. When we arrived at the Community Church, we were greeted warmly by Georgina and Stephen who introduced us to the Pastor, Pat Murphy. Pat told us that for a long time now he had felt that the sad and bloody history of Wexford had affected the town and its people. "It's like a dark cloud hanging over us," he said. There's that dark cloud again, and I remembered Isaiah 60, and John Mulinde's prophecy.

People from many different denominations came together that

night to hear what we had to say. Each place was different and we were never sure how people would respond, but once again we were overwhelmed. Afterwards, we had an opportunity to talk with some of the folk. This is always a fruitful time, just to listen to the different stories they had to tell. One gentleman named Des, stands out in particular, he was a real character. Des was a 68-year-old Catholic man who had been through a rough time and lost everything before he became a Christian. Because of this experience, he knew for himself the power of healing deep wounds and although he had only been a Christian a short time, he understood exactly what our visit was all about. "I believe" he said "that because you have come in obedience, a great healing has already happened in the town."

Afterwards, as I was talking to Pat Murphy, I began to feel a little uncomfortable. He was so enthusiastic and said that he felt it was important to gather as many people as possible and make this a big event in September. I knew I had to be honest with him. I didn't want to give him or anyone else the wrong impression. "Pat," I said "as yet I haven't talked to any leaders back home and have no idea who, if anyone, will come with me. I'm a bit worried that you might plan this big event and then find only myself and a few others turning up in the autumn." Pat looked at me and smiled, and then he spoke this word to me:

> "Shirley, you are specially chosen for this very significant task. The Lord has looked at your heart and He sees that you are the one that He himself has kept for this day and time of reconciliation. Ephesians 1 v 3-4 tells us that God knew you before the foundations of the world. 1 Samuel 17 tells that God looked upon the heart. He sees your heart Shirley and knew you before the world was made. He then and there made a decision to keep you throughout all generations until this day. God has a calling and a plan for you before the foundation of the world. Therefore as He knew you and saw your heart He singled you out of all generations

and peoples for a unique job and call. This choice carries with it a responsibility of submission and obedience and that is why you are His special one whom He could trust with this call. "

I didn't know what to say, I felt so inadequate. Yet I knew that God had prepared me for this time and by His grace and through Christ, all things are possible. Pat wrote the words down so that I could think and pray about them when I returned home. This proved to be a good idea, as many times, whenever I have doubted myself and my calling, I have looked again at what God said. Psalm 139 speaks of an all-knowing God. He knows when we sit and when we rise. He knew us before we were born. Verse 16 says, "*All the days ordained to me were written in your book before one of them came to be.*" Therefore, you and I are no accident, but part of God's amazing plan. He had me in mind when He created all things, just as He had you in mind too. I came to realise that I was born at exactly the right time for His purposes.

Why am I sharing this with you? Well, maybe there is someone reading this who is going through a time of doubt and who thinks that God has made a mistake. I want you to know God doesn't make mistakes and you are in good company if you doubt yourself. Gideon, in Judges 6 v 15, called himself, "*the least in my family.*" However, the angel of God knew different and called him, "*mighty warrior*" (v12). Moses didn't believe in himself either. After murdering an Egyptian, he escaped into the desert where he stayed for many years. Then suddenly, God speaks to him from a burning bush. I have often wondered what people would think if the same thing should happen today! Look where that led Moses, he finished up leading God's people to freedom.

God knows His plan for each of our lives and He also knows what needs to change. So even though it may be hard to believe, just trust the one who raised Jesus from death to life, because He is a God of the impossible. If you find yourself having difficulty believing what God has said, or that He could use you, well take it from me, He does and He will. However, it's not because you are perfect, or because you have proved your worth, it's because of His grace and love to you and those whom He will touch through you. 2 Corinthians 4 v 7 says, *"But we have this treasure in jars of clay to show that this all surpassing power is from God."* Amazingly, God chooses to use us, but let us never forget that the all-surpassing power is from Him!

Georgina, bless her, had been true to her promise. She had arranged a meeting the following day with the Guardian from the Franciscan Friary and the local Catholic Priest. Although regrettably she had to work, Stephen said that he would be joining us. Des, who overheard our conversation, asked if we would mind if he came too. We were warmly welcomed and after introductions, I gave a quick overview of the vision. I wasn't surprised, but I was sorry that they had difficulty seeing where we were coming from. Not that they were opposed to the idea, but they just couldn't see what good it would do. Des asked if he could speak, "This is a spiritual battle," he said "and we need to see it through spiritual eyes." He continued to say this was no different to Pope John Paul II asking for forgiveness from the Jews on behalf of the Catholic Church. I didn't want to put them in a difficult position, so I just said that we would abide by their decision. In the end, they agreed that the walk would do no harm and neither of them had any objections to it. In fact, the Priest said that he couldn't be there himself, but he was very happy for a service to be held in his church. Before we left, both men blessed us and encouraged us to contact Huntingdon Town Council, as well as the churches, for their endorsement of our walk. This had been a very different meeting to the one the previous night, but we knew that, yet again, God had gone before us. We thanked both Des and Stephen for their support and encouragement and so with a tremendous sense of peace, we headed towards our next destination, Waterford.

We arrived in Tramore, outside Waterford, and met up with Patricia Finnerty (a friend of Paddy Monaghan's in Dublin) and her friend Lynn. Straight away it was obvious to us that both these ladies had a real longing for God to bring His healing to their land. As I finished sharing our vision, Patricia, with tears in her eyes said, "While you were talking, I had a picture of you pouring oil on the land and a huge wave was coming behind you." She said it reminded her of a vision that many people in Ireland had seen before, of a dam bursting over the land. As soon as she said this, she started to weep. My heart went out to her. I felt that God was showing us that the dam bursting would be the release of all the pain and tears that have built up over the years.

Later, she told us that during Cromwell's time, her family, like so many, had been robbed of their land and inheritance. "Sometimes," she said "it's almost as if the struggle is still going on." Oh Lord, please forgive us! After a time of prayer, and promises from both ladies that they would contact leaders and pastors in their area, we went on our way.

We followed their directions into Waterford and soon found the guest house where we were staying that night. We pulled off the road and climbed up a steep incline that twisted its way through the shrubs. What a fantastic view we had as we pulled into the drive at the top! The house looked out over the river and the city of Waterford, it was breathtaking. We lay in bed that night with the curtains drawn back, not needing to say a word as we gazed out of the window at the magnificent view. The next morning, we had a look around the house and the owner told us that it had been standing for many centuries, even in the time of Cromwell. A guidebook lay on the coffee table, and together with the pictures on the wall, it gave us some knowledge of the history of Waterford during Cromwell's time. You could see that this was a very strategic place with a prosperous trading port. No wonder Cromwell had wanted to capture it!

To our surprise, down in the city centre, a long stretch of the city wall is still standing despite many onslaughts in the past, and a cannon ball from one of Cromwell's attacks is still lodged in one of the towers. We also discovered the city's Latin motto meant "No surrender." It refers to the fact that they had not surrendered to Oliver Cromwell, as other towns had done, something they are still very proud of to this day. However, the town did fall to his son-in-law a year later. We had hoped to see the Town Clerk, but unfortunately no one was available to speak to us, as the officials were busy with the referendum. We had enjoyed our visit, even though we were disappointed not to make more contacts. As Cromwell made no in-roads in Waterford, was this history repeating itself?

It was late afternoon when we reached Cork. After a meeting that evening, we met a lady outside the venue who seemed a little upset that she had missed our introduction and went on to ask if we were from England. We introduced ourselves and I told her about the proposed Cromwell walk. She was very interested and wanted to know how on earth we came to be doing something like this. We invited her back to our room where she listened with great excitement as I told her our story. By the time I had finished, she was quite overwhelmed and desperately wanted to be involved. She went on to tell us about a group led by a Sister Bridget who had plans to pray around the city walls that very week. She was sure this was a connection God wanted us to make.

So the next day, we made our way to the Prayer Centre to meet Sister Bridget. She gave us a hearty welcome and was desperate to hear more about our proposed plans. Once again, like the lady the day before, her excitement grew as she listened to the story and even more so when I came to the Annette part, where I was lifted out with "a net". "I know this is of God," she said. We were amazed at the certainty of her response. "What makes you so sure?" I asked her. She went on to share about a dream she'd had. In it she saw two trays on a table each covered with a tea towel. She approached the table and lifted up the first tea towel. Underneath she saw lots of small birds and a sign over them saying "Quail". She went on, "I kept this dream to myself until recently, when one morning at the Prayer Meeting, one of our gentlemen got up to leave and as he did so, he turned around and said, "We have had the Manna, now God is sending us Quail." Katie, Phyllis and I could hardly believe our ears. You see, the amazing thing is that Annette's surname is Quail! God wanted this faithful lady to know that this was Him. Sister Bridget was so encouraged by our visit that she promised to inform people from other churches in the area. We left feeling very humbled by this lovely lady with a huge heart.

Our next stop was the City Hall. Unfortunately once again we were unable to meet with the Town Clerk but his secretary was very interested in what we had to say and encouraged us to write to him. I often wonder what the people in the offices thought about us. Perhaps they thought we were a bit crazy! If I didn't know the full story and how God has led us, I might even think that myself!

We headed off on the longest drive of our trip to Athlone, in the heart of Ireland. Athlone is key as it was one of the places where the Catholic people were herded across the river to the west of Ireland. With the end in sight, we looked forward to relaxing and meeting up again with Trevor and Diane Hill, leaders of the River of Life Church. I had met this couple previously. They have been through some very tough times yet their love and care for others never ceases. That evening as we were finishing our meal, the doorbell rang. It was a neighbour who had come to hear what our visit was all about.

As we sat talking, I could see she had a problem with the vision. She couldn't see the need to open up old wounds. However, as we shared a little more, she began to open up and tell us her own story. "I don't really understand why, but all my life I have been angry towards the English and it's not just me, this has affected my whole family." As she continued to share, she began to see the root of her own feelings. All those years ago during the Civil War, her family too had been robbed of their land and inheritance. No wonder she was angry! I explained that like so many people, her anger had been locked away inside for years. Our prayer is that as we acknowledge their pain and say we are sorry, it will enable her and others to release the hurt and allow Jesus to bring healing and then maybe they will be able to forgive. She turned to me and put her hand on mine, "Shirley, would you pray for me please, I want to be rid of this anger forever." We spent time in repentance and prayer, asking Jesus to heal this deep wound. He was so gracious to her that evening and I felt very privileged to be a witness. She got up to leave and as she was about to go through the door she turned and said, "Praise God, I am now sure that your trip is a good idea after all!"

We were now near the end of our time in Ireland and once again, I felt a bit sad at the thought of leaving. Over breakfast on that last morning, I shared our vision with our hostess She responded, "Do you know for years now, I too have had a vision. In it I can see Irish people coming home in their hundreds and thousands and following behind them is a huge tidal wave covering the whole of Ireland". This reminded me of the book "Operation Exodus", the story of the Jews returning home. As we left that day, I pondered on this thought. I had a wonderful sense of God's love for the people of Ireland. I believe that the Cromwell part of their history is very much on His heart. One day I am sure that like a wave, the Holy Spirit will come and the love of Jesus will wash over this land and bring His healing.

Chapter Twelve

You are the Letter

Our time in Ireland had been remarkable, far beyond anything we could have imagined and any doubts about our proposed trip had been laid to rest. This part of history and the Irish people were definitely on God's agenda. So, with that assurance it was time to contact both the Church and Civic authorities. The thought of facing the Town Clerk in Huntingdon threw me into a panic. I could see why the Irish agreed to the idea of healing the past, because they were the injured party, but in Huntingdon it was different. I so much wanted to help them realise that it isn't only for Ireland's benefit, it's for ours in Huntingdon too.

I was so nervous as we entered the Council offices. I had prayed for this time for years, and now it was here. I was reminded of 2 Corinthians 12 v 9, when God says "*My grace is sufficient for you, for my power is made perfect in weakness.*" However, we were soon to realise that God had prepared the way, as the then Town Clerk was an avid lover of Ireland. He was also very interested to hear of Katie's connections in Drogheda and this opened the way for us to share the vision. I finished by saying, "We thought we should inform you and the Council of our intentions and hopefully get support from the town." It would be unfair to say that he understood straight away, as he himself had never experienced any problems. However, he could see that this was a good idea and thought the town should be involved.

The next hurdle, meeting with Huntingdon Churches Together, I found more difficult in some ways. We needed their support and if possible, a letter of apology. I was soon to realise that I was worrying more about my own reputation than being obedient to God. Our Pastor had the idea of producing a draft letter. "This way" he said, "they would have something to work from." I agreed and thankfully he took this task on.

The chairman for the year was the local Catholic Priest. This seemed rather appropriate! After I shared the vision, he asked if anyone had any comments. As I expected, there were quite a few, some positive, while others were unsure. "After all," one clergy said "if it wasn't for Cromwell, we wouldn't have religious freedom." This shows the complexity of the subject. "We have never denied the good things that Cromwell accomplished," I said, "but we do have to own the things done in the name of Christ that were wrong. If we don't, we are condoning what the people in Ireland and elsewhere have suffered. After all, they are our brothers and sisters too."

One story that came out of the subsequent church meetings was of a gentleman who had made a recent visit to America. He said that his association was linked with Cromwell, so when he presented the hosts with a banner which had a picture of Cromwell on, it was received with gratitude and hung up. However later, when a Catholic Priest got up to speak, he walked over to where the banner was and said, "It's no good, I cannot speak with that man looking at me." And he turned the banner over! Just seeing a picture of Cromwell still affected him deeply. This is the wound that God wants to heal.

The letter from the ministers did take a little longer than we expected, but I was overjoyed when I received a telephone call from the chairman asking to see me. Vanessa and I arrived at his home a little nervous, but that nervousness soon turned to excitement as we were shown the final letter. "It's taken a while, but are you happy with it?" he said. I was happy, very happy!

As we watched him putting his name to this very special document, I was reminded of the letters of authority that Nehemiah needed. The Priest turned and handed it to me, adding his blessing as he did so. The next thing now was to get the signatures of all the other ministers. When the letter was complete, we had it photocopied and framed. We did this because we felt it was important not only to take the letter to every town, but also to leave it behind as our gift to each church and civic leader. The original copy was later framed and presented to Bertie Ahern, the then Taoiseach (Prime Minister) of the Irish Republic.

During this time, the Town Clerk in Huntingdon arranged for us to meet with the Town Council. Although everything seemed to go well that night, I received a letter a few days later saying that at this time they didn't feel able to send a letter of apology. I could understand their reasons. Although some councillors agreed with the need to say sorry for Cromwell's actions, it was also felt that because this was such a complex subject, they couldn't speak on behalf of the whole town. However, they did agree that a letter from the churches was appropriate.

With these two meetings out of the way now, we asked "what next Lord?" I was reminded of a dream I had had a few weeks ago. In it, I was sitting writing a letter to the Prime Minister, and on the same day, Vanessa woke with the words "Write to top authority". Although I was nervous about this, I had no doubt that this was the right thing to do. The Civil War had affected the whole of the country. Cromwell was the country's leader of that day and therefore Tony Blair, as leader of our Government then, should know what was going on. We felt it was important to respect those in authority. This idea grew the more we prayed about it. We soon realised that it wasn't just the Prime Minister that we should inform, but all leaders, both political and church, Protestant and Catholic, here and in Ireland.

The letter writing was a mammoth task, and a daunting one too! Because of my dyslexia (word blindness), I had a real fear of writing, so I was glad to have Vanessa as a co-worker. If this task wasn't daunting enough, you can imagine how Vanessa felt when I told her that for many years, I had been aware that we should also write to the Queen and now seemed to be the right time! I wanted to tell her Majesty not only about our journey, but more importantly, to apologise for the actions of Cromwell. The Monarch in 1649 was

King Charles I, and he was accused of treason, found guilty and beheaded. I felt prompted by God to address the issue in this the Queen's Jubilee year.

Before we began to write this letter, Vanessa and I spent time in prayer. I had the words "the pen of a ready writer," in my head. I couldn't remember exactly where it came from, but I was sure it was from the Psalms. So we began to search the scriptures, and it wasn't long before we found Psalm 45. No wonder our attention had been drawn to this. We felt sure this was yet another confirmation when we read that this Psalm was written as a poem to the King. So, in July 2002, the letter informing the Queen of our Cromwell Reconciliation Journey was written. We also took the opportunity to apologise to her as the present Monarch, saying how sorry we were that Cromwell, who was from our town, was responsible for the death of a previous Monarch, King Charles I. We concluded our letter by congratulating her on her Jubilee and blessing her as our Queen.

Within days of writing, I received a reply from 10 Downing Street. It thanked me for informing the Prime Minister of our reconciliation journey and said that the points we made would be carefully considered. It ended by saying, "Mr Blair has asked me to send you his very best wishes to all concerned with your journey." We were thrilled to have the blessing of the top authority in our land. This letter seemed to open the floodgates and over the next few weeks, we received many more, each blessing us for what we were doing.

However, the icing on the cake for us was when we later received a reply from Buckingham Palace. The letter expressed the Queen's regret for the delay in replying, and sent her good wishes to all who took part in the Reconciliation Journey. It continued to say that the Queen had read our letter and appreciated our thoughtfulness in writing to express our views on the action of Cromwell. This was what we needed to hear, that the Queen herself had read our letter of apology. Thank you God!

As our trip was drawing closer, we knew that we had a daunting task ahead of us, so we set more time aside for prayer and fasting. One day as I was praying, the words "You are the letter." popped into my mind. Where did that come from? I wondered. Then it happened again, "You are the letter." I tried to dismiss this, I told myself it was only because I had spent so much time thinking about the letters we had sent out recently. Then I turned to my Bible notes. The study for that day was 2 Corinthians chapter 3 v 1-6. I read verse 2; *"You yourselves are the letter, written on our hearts, known and read by everybody. You show that you are a letter from Christ, the result of our ministry, written not in ink but with the Spirit of the living God, not on tablets of stone but on tablets of human hearts."* I remembered John Mulinde's teaching from way back, when he said "If you go to hurting people and talk of God's love, they won't hear about the love, but they will remember what your people had done to them." I knew that the letter from the churches played a very important part in the healing process as it carried love and repentance for their pain. However, I also realised I was the letter that people would read. How we behaved and what we carried was very important, and any hypocrisy would soon be spotted.

That evening as we gathered for prayer God gave us a picture of a fire burning and cleansing the land of Ireland. Annette remembered that a recent bush fire in America had been started by the burning of a letter. I told them of my day and what I felt God was saying. We all agreed that as we were going ourselves, not just sending the letter, but putting our feet to the ground and our faith into action, it was this that would speak volumes to the Irish people.

As a family, we were to be tested over these months. It started when my eldest son returned home after the break-up of his marriage. The pain of that time is still with me as I watched him cope with the knowledge that his two small children were now 300 miles away. I often wished he was small again and I could pick him up and hug the pain away, but that's not possible when they are six-foot-three and grown up! We also missed Amy and Elli, as we were used to having them just around the corner.

Alison, our daughter, was also going through a bad time. Her baby daughter, Adele, became very ill and was admitted to hospital with suspected meningitis. That was so hard on everyone, not only to see our little girl suffering, but also watching her Mummy and Daddy suffer too. We alerted the whole prayer network and praise God, she made a good recovery. On top of all this, my husband Tony, who was already in poor health, started to complain about his throat. Within a few days, he was diagnosed with a severe throat infection. Well at least that's what we all thought it was at the time, though it turned out to be more than that later on.

If that wasn't enough, the pain I was experiencing in my shoulder increased. So much so that I was unable to raise my arm very far, which became increasingly frustrating as it restricted what I could do. I made an appointment to see a specialist and after a scan, I was told that I needed an operation. The timing for this couldn't be worse. "Lord please do something," I cried. He did!

One Sunday evening, I attended one of the town's joint celebrations. The topic was God's healing, but I was in so much pain that I found it hard to concentrate. So, when an invitation for prayer was given, I didn't hesitate to go forward. I remember that evening as if it was yesterday. The Pastor from one the churches in the town came towards me. After telling him what the problem was, he gently placed his hand upon my shoulder and prayed. At first, I didn't feel anything, but that never bothers me, as often people don't. However, after a short time, my hands and arms started to tingle. This gently increased until it was like electric shocks going up and down each arm. He continued to pray for my total healing. He then went on to ask God to anoint the work He had called me to do for the next 20, 30, or 40 years! That very evening my shoulder was totally healed, and Praise God, to this day I have never needed that operation.

During this preparation time, we couldn't believe how many programmes were broadcast on television about the Civil War and in particular, Cromwell's exploits in Ireland. I found it fascinating to listen to the historians describing this time as a very bloody part of history and how they believed that this was much more than a Civil War. It was, they said, a religious war. The same words that God had given to us all those months ago! This was very encouraging!

With only weeks to go, the telephone hardly seemed to stop ringing with people enquiring about the trip. I hadn't realised the word was getting around so much, until I received a call from Irish radio asking if I would speak about our journey on their midday show. I panicked, as I remembered the days long ago when I used to record Christian messages for a telephone ministry. I was so nervous before each session that I used to dry up half way through. What if that happened again? I felt God's gentle reassuring touch as I remembered His word in Joshua 1 v 5b "*I will never leave you, nor forsake you. Be strong and courageous.*" This was to be the first of many radio broadcasts.

One day, I received a call from Harry Smith at the Rostrevor Christian Renewal Centre in Northern Ireland. He told me that during their prayer time, they had had a real sense of God weeping over the land of Ireland. He went on to say that the bloodshed in the time of Cromwell had put a curse on the land for more blood to be shed. Hosea 4 v 2b-3a, "*Bloodshed follows bloodshed, because of this the land mourns.*" It was felt that what we were about to do was going to reverse the curse and they pledged to continue to pray for us. It was such a good feeling to know that we were in partnership together.

Summer had passed and it was September again and the time for us to leave was drawing close. I heard from Robin and Margaret that they wanted to come and pray with us. I was thrilled! This couple had prayed with me every time I went off on a WTC course, and here they were doing the same again. However, there was more to it this time. God had given Robin the scripture Isaiah 60 v 1-3 (*Arise, shine, for your light has come …*) while he was a Minister in Huntingdon, and so I had felt for a long time that God had birthed this plan for reconciliation through him many years ago. So the following week when we gathered together, I was thrilled to hear Robin say that what had been birthed then, would now grow in Ireland. He anointed us individually, and God spoke these reassuring words to us:

> "Don't worry about what you are going to say. I will put my words in your mouth. Don't worry about what you will wear, or what you will eat, because I will be with you. Don't worry about the transport, I have it in my hands. My glory is in you and will shine through you and will be seen by others."

With hugs and tears, we left that night knowing that we had received a tremendous blessing and were fully prepared for the task ahead. To make things complete, I received telephone calls from the Rev Edward Wright (the gentleman we met in London whose ancestor fought with Cromwell) and our friend Rev Stephen Talbot from Ashburnham. They both told me that they planned to come with us for the first few days and would meet up with us at Rostrevor, where we planned to have a day's rest and preparation before the start of the Reconciliation Journey. It filled me with awe to know that God was putting everything in place for the journey ahead of us.

Chapter Thirteen
Retracing Cromwell's Steps

The day of our departure arrived and I woke with a real excitement and expectation. Many people had warned me that the Irish Sea was a particularly rough stretch of water and this could easily have worried me, but thankfully it didn't. God had said in that prophecy back in 1990 that "There would be a significant crossing point, a point of no return," and I felt this was that crossing point. So I was going to trust Him. He didn't let us down, the journey was so smooth that I almost forgot I was onboard a ship. The following day, someone asked the question, "How was the crossing over?" I caught Vanessa's eye, we both knew what the other was thinking. "Crossing over" that was what we had done, and this was now the point of no return that God had spoken of in that very first prophetic word all those years before.

Many times during the planning of this trip we were given the scripture from Isaiah 62 v 10, "*Pass through, pass through the gates! Prepare the way for the people. Build up, build up the highway! Remove the stones. Raise a banner for the nations.*" Later on when Stephen and Edward arrived, we gathered for prayer and once again this scripture was given. This time though, because it came from someone totally different, it was very confirming. What we didn't know then was how appropriate this scripture was for Drogheda.

Before you embark on something like this, it's important that you make sure that anything that could possibly hinder what God wants to do should be brought before Him and dealt with. So with this in mind, I took my bottle of oil and started to pray and anoint each person in turn. When I came to Edward, I asked Katie if she would pray for him. I felt this was very important knowing both their backgrounds. Katie has Irish Catholic roots and her family are from Drogheda and Edward is a descendant of a man from Cromwell's army. I will always remember Katie's response as she approached him, saying "It will be a great pleasure and honour." As she prayed, Edward just started to weep. This was to be a prophetic picture for us, Edward on his knees weeping, as he repented on behalf of his family and Katie hugging him as she forgave him on behalf of hers. No one moved for a time, we didn't want to break this special moment. We just wanted to stay in the presence of God.

I had been asked to speak at a meeting that evening and share how this reconciliation journey had come about. After I had finished, Annette rose to her feet. I was quite surprised, because being a quiet person this isn't something she would normally do. Annette told everyone how she had been asking God questions like "What difference was this going to make to the people of Northern Ireland? And what are we doing here anyway, when we are supposed to be going to the Republic? She went on, "As I was thinking about this, I saw a clear picture of a map of Ireland with a bottle of oil tipped over. The oil was pouring out from the North and flowing into the South." She felt God was saying that this was where the healing was coming from the North and into the South. I heard someone gasp. One of the ladies present came forward and said that before she left home that evening, she felt prompted to put a bottle of oil in her bag. What confirmation! Edward then picked up his shofar (ram's horn) and started to blow. The sound that came out was quite haunting and sent shivers my spine. It was a time of celebrating what God was about to do.

Afterwards, Carl Anderson, a pastor visiting from Minnesota, USA, came to speak to me. He had heard about our reconciliation journey, and felt that it was important to come and hear the story for himself. He went on, "I feel God has given me some words for you, but I need to go away and check this out before sharing them." I respected him for this. "However," he continued "if it's what God wants, I would like to come and share them tomorrow morning before you leave on this journey." "That would be fine," I replied and invited him to join our prayer time. I went to bed that night with a real expectation in my spirit.

The long-awaited September 11th 2002 arrived. Exactly 353 years to the day that Cromwell first entered Drogheda. I woke with very mixed feelings. I was excited, but also quite nervous. "Dear Lord," I prayed "I have waited so long for this and I know I can trust you to fulfil all that you have promised. Help me to do my part in a way that is acceptable to you."

As we met together for morning prayers, there was a real air of excitement and anticipation. I was pleased to see Carl too. After introducing him to the team, I invited him to share what God had laid on his heart. He began "Last night, I felt God impressing on me that this journey of yours is all about reclaiming the land." This was a good start, as it was in tune with what God had said to us previously. "This land was built by God's people, Saint Patrick and others. Over time, stones have been placed on the highway through sin. However, God was preparing the highway again." He quoted Isaiah 62 v 10, *"Pass through, pass through the gates! Prepare the way for the people! Build up, build up the highway! Remove the stones! Raise a banner for the nations!"* We looked at each other in amazement. He continued. "The highway was green but the stones are in the way and need to be cleared, then the wells will spring up. Joshua 1 v 3, *"I will give you every place you set your foot."* This is the year of Jubilee, of giving back the land." He went on, "Repentance and forgiveness are necessary for healing, and the battle is over the land. You must identify with the sins of the past; generational curses, spoken curses and blood curses. There will be a simultaneous reconciliation and reclaiming of the land as you proclaim, "We reclaim this land for the glory and kingdom of God." It will be a spiritual reuniting of the land and Jesus. You need to use the sword of the Spirit, the Rhema word of God. The enemy will try to attack and steal back what's been gained, but the Holy Spirit will give you scriptures for each place, so that the victory can be maintained. Give these words to the intercessors in that place so that they can continue to pray them over their land."

He went on to say that before he left America, he was given a bottle of oil from Brownsville. This oil had been specifically set aside for reclaiming the land and he wanted to anoint our feet before we set off. We were blown away, as every word confirmed what God had already said to us. Without doubt, this was God.

There was a wonderful sense of God's presence as he humbly knelt at the feet of each person, and as he did, he was given a specific word and role for each of us. One person was given the gift of prophecy; one anointing for breakthrough, to break bondages; one was given authority over strongholds; and others were given a ministry in reconciliation. The word for Phyllis, I remember, was that she was to be the remnant left behind to show what God has done and for the healing of the wound. This was a truly amazing start to the day!

After a blessing from Harry Smith and folk at the Renewal Centre, we set off not knowing what the day ahead had in store. We had only been travelling a short while, when the phone rang. It was Irish Radio telling me that an interview that had been arranged would take place in about two minutes time. The interview was a three-way conversation between Frank Godfrey, former mayor of Drogheda, Tom Reilly, author of "*Cromwell; An Honourable Enemy*" and myself. We hadn't been on the air long before it became clear that Tom Reilly wasn't happy with us at all. I could understand why. He felt that because Huntingdon Town Council had not sent a representative, the whole thing was a waste of time, "an empty gesture" he called it. Frank Godfrey, however, could see that this was an expression of love and said that he welcomed Arise Ministries with open arms. I was asked to comment. I remember saying that I completely understood what Tom Reilly felt, but it wasn't about who came, but it was about saying sorry for something that happened on this very day in 1649. I continued "Not only are we retracing the route Cromwell had taken, but we are waiting outside each place to be invited in, which is the opposite of what was done back in history." After the interview was over, I gave a deep sigh of relief, but I felt a little sad. Why can't people just accept the love this journey brings?

The drive to Drogheda didn't take long and soon we were on the outskirts of town. We were met by two gentlemen from the Holy Family prayer group who escorted us to the Monastery of St. Catherine of Siena, where we were to stay. On arrival, we were introduced to Sister Regina, a very gracious and lovely lady, who, along with the big electric gates outside, was to play an important part in our story. We quickly unloaded the cars and set off again, to attend a reception with the Mayor at a local hotel.

We were introduced to Councillor Malachy Godfrey, the Mayor of Drogheda, and Councillor Frank Godfrey (the former Mayor who had earlier been on the radio). Our time together began with the reading of Psalm 133, *"How good and pleasant it is when brothers dwell in unity ... for there the Lord bestows a blessing."* This scripture encouraged us all enormously. I remember feeling rather nervous, not knowing how things were going to proceed, when I had one of the greatest surprises of the day. I was presented with a beautiful engraved crystal bowl from the Holy Family group and an illustrated book about Drogheda from the Mayor. It just hadn't occurred to me that this would happen. As the Mayor made his presentation, he welcomed us all to the town and said that our coming was a wonderful gesture of good will. When it was my turn, I addressed the Mayor first, thanking him for his kind words of welcome and also thanked everyone for their hospitality. This was the time to present the letters, I thought. I had no idea how I was going to do this, it wasn't something I had rehearsed. So, after explaining to everyone what the journey was all about, I read the letter aloud;

> "We, the members of Churches Together in Huntingdon, warmly greet our brothers and sisters in the churches and

towns of Drogheda, Wexford and elsewhere in Ireland. We want you to know that in our hearts we fully support the reconciliation, Christian love and fellowship that this walk represents.

Our town has for many years been associated with Oliver Cromwell. In the local churches, we recognise the pain his coming to Ireland meant and still means. For this we are deeply sorry. Our hope is that through this walk we will share time and prayer together, which will show the unity for which our Saviour prayed.

May the Lord bless you and bring you peace. May your lovely land know his abundant blessing."

As I passed the letter over to the Mayor, I apologised to him for Cromwell's actions and said that the letter was an expression of love and regret from the churches in Huntingdon for the pain Cromwell had caused the town. He received it gratefully. I then asked Father Kiery, affectionately known as Father Paddy, to join me. What happened next I still find amazing and very moving to recall. Before presenting him with his copy of the letter, I asked him to forgive the death and destruction that the Catholic people had suffered. This he did without hesitation. I handed him the letter, touching his arm as I did so. Immediately, I began to weep. Not just a tear or two, no, I wept, something I don't do easily. Father Paddy put his arms around me and just held me tight, not trying to stop the tears. The love and acceptance I felt at that moment I can't even begin to explain, but I felt very humbled by this man's grace.

Katie and Edward joined us. Edward was in tears as he repented on behalf of his forebears for their part in the destruction of Drogheda. Katie wept, as her family were part of the history here too. It was a lovely moment as Father Paddy took hold of both their hands and pronounced peace over them and their families. Afterwards I was told that many others were also touched, both by the tears and by this expression of God's love as we held each other in forgiveness.

Before lunch, we were escorted around the town and onto St Mary's Church, which has been converted into The Heritage Centre. We walked past the church and on through the graveyard, to the back of the grounds. It was here that Cromwell and his men entered Drogheda. We lingered for a while, looking out over the surrounding wall. You could easily imagine the events of that day long ago as Cromwell ordered the assault, intending to gain St Mary's Church as a foothold into the town. After a fierce battle and great loss of life, he managed to breach the walls right where we were standing. We gathered together, asking God to forgive all the bloodshed. I took the oil and poured some over the land, knowing that only God can heal this deep wound. On the way back, an elderly lady called out from her doorway, "You are very welcome here, very welcome indeed." "Thank you" I replied. As someone who feels a burden for what Cromwell has done, being welcomed here meant a lot. This was, I believe, a sign from God, telling us that the healing had begun.

Over lunch one lady shared how she hadn't planned to attend the meeting that morning. "However," she went on "I am so glad I did. I have never experienced anything like this before, it was so beautiful. I couldn't believe how it affected me, but when you started to cry and Father Paddy held you, I was in tears too." She said that this day had given her hope for the future and she recommitted her life to Jesus. Praise the Lord!

That afternoon we also visited St Peter's Anglican Church, where it is reported that people hid from Cromwell's soldiers in the tower. Cromwell ordered wood to be piled up underneath the tower and set alight. Everyone died, they were unable to escape. What we didn't know was that they had just finished refurbishing the church after yet another fire. It was quite a strange feeling as we gathered for prayer with the Minister, still able to smell the burning. The scripture that was given for them was Isaiah 61, *"The Spirit of the Sovereign Lord is on me, … to comfort all who mourn, and provide for those who grieve in Zion to bestow on them a crown of beauty instead of ashes, the oil of gladness instead of mourning, and a garment of praise, instead of a spirit of despair."* We finished up at Mill Mount, a monument set high on the hill overlooking the town. We were told this was where the Royalist governor Sir Arthur Aston, made his last stand against Cromwell.

On returning to the Monastery, we reflected over all that had happened during the day, and we couldn't help but notice how many times "gates" were mentioned. Even the crystal bowl that had been presented to us was engraved with the famous St Lawrence's Gate. As we thought about this, I remembered being told that Drogheda was once known as the "Gateway to mission". "What was that scripture God had given us again this morning?" I said. "*Pass through, pass through the gates.*" (Isaiah 62 v 10). It goes on, "*Prepare a way for the people. Remove the stones.*" I believe that the pain of this time in history, when the gates had to be closed to protect the town against Cromwell's invasion, is one of the stones that needed to be removed, so that, through forgiveness, the gates of mission can be opened again. So this is what we prayed, "Open wide the gates Lord, open wide the gates and let your Kingdom in!"

We were going to the Holy Family's prayer meeting that evening, and before we left, Sister Regina warned me about the electric gates. She said they were on a timer and normally they close at nine, but tonight it had been extended to ten o'clock. "However, be warned," she said "they will close on time and once they're closed, they won't open again until morning." I was very conscious of this as I rose to speak that night. I cut it as short as possible, just telling them the main parts of the story, including the picture I had of the one-legged man.

The evening turned out to be another very emotional time, as we again repented for the past, and hugs of forgiveness were given. Time ran out on us and unfortunately we were unable to stay and chat over refreshments. It was gone ten o'clock when we approached the Monastery, and we were all worried that the gates would be closed. You can imagine the relief as we turned the corner and found them still open.

During breakfast the following morning, Sister Regina arrived. "My dear, what did you pray yesterday?" she asked me excitedly, "Last night no matter what we did we couldn't close the gates! We tried everything but they just wouldn't close!" She went on, "We are so excited and believe God has given us a sign that our prayers have been answered and the gates are now open wide for His Spirit to flow through this land!" We could hardly believe our ears! God you are so amazing! She then took hold of my hand, "Thank you for coming," she said "we know God has sent you all." I felt very humbled knowing that the Sisters here had sacrificed their lives to prayer. "All we are doing," I said "is adding our little bit to your many prayers, and that has been a real privilege."

We had a wonderful prayer time that morning, declaring Psalm 24 v 7-10 over this town:

Lift up your heads, O you gates; be lifted up, you ancient doors, that the King of glory may come in.
Who is this King of glory?
The Lord strong and mighty, the Lord mighty in battle.
Lift up your heads, O you gates; lift them up, you ancient doors, that the King of glory may come in.
Who is he, this King of glory?
The Lord Almighty he is the King of glory.

After this, we couldn't think of a better place to start our prayer walk than at St Lawrence's Gate. Katie was most excited as this is only a stone's throw away from where her family lived. When we arrived, we were a little disappointed to find the gate covered with scaffolding and in the process of being restored. However, we realised that this was a perfect picture of what God was doing - restoring the gates of mission.

We hadn't been there long when a Monsignor came by. He stopped and asked us what we were doing. When we told him we were praying, he replied "Really? I didn't think you could possibly be doing that, you all look too happy!" We laughed. I went on to tell him about our visit to Drogheda, before asking him if he would like to join us. He replied by saying that he would love too. I am so glad he did, because on our return to England we were informed that the Monsignor had died suddenly, shortly after our visit.

Our time at the gate was very powerful, and hard to describe. After prayers of confession, Edward expressed his desire to wash Katie's feet in an act of penitence for his family's part in the war. We hadn't planned to do this, but there we were, in full view of everyone, taking turns to wash each other's feet. Representatives of Cromwell's army were washing the feet of representatives of the Irish people and not only with water, but also with tears.

During this time, we were joined by a lady from the Holy Family Catholic Church. She recognised us from the previous day. She stopped to ask for prayer, as she had just heard she was to have another operation for cancer the following week. Stephen gently placed his hand on her head and as he anointed her with oil, we all prayed for a miracle. We could tell that God had been faithful to His word, because it was obvious to us that He met with her there on the street. The following year when we returned to Drogheda, we saw this lady again. This time she was able to tell us that she hadn't needed that operation, as the cancer had disappeared and she was completely healed! Praise God!

To finish our time at St Lawrence's gate, we decided that it would be good to proclaim the scripture "*Pass through, pass through the gates. Build up, build up the highway. Remove the stones. Raise a banner for the nations.*" We felt God had shown us that He was removing stones that had blocked His way for centuries. At that very moment, a workman appeared carrying a huge stone, which he had just carried down from the top of the gateway! It was a physical confirmation of what God was doing! Over the road, another workman stood watching a little bemused at what we were doing, so Katie went over to talk to him. He was very interested and said that if more people cared like this, the world might be a better place!

In the evening, we met up again with a few people, including Father Paddy. He saw us arriving in the car park and came rushing over to greet us, waving a sheet of paper in his hand. "I'm so glad to see you again," he said "I wanted to show you this. You said that God led you to Ireland by showing you a picture of a man with only one leg. Well, what do you think of this?" He passed me the piece of paper. It was a page that he had photocopied from a book, telling the story of how Sir Arthur Aston had defended the town in 1649. He lost the battle and finished up being beaten to death with his own wooden leg! I was lost for words and felt very reassured that this was God's work.

Before leaving we planned to give the Sisters one of the framed letters as a reminder of what God had done. However, Sister Regina surprised me first. She appeared in the doorway with a beautiful bouquet of roses, picked from their garden. I just stood in disbelief, how much more was God going to give me? These roses reminded me of the rose God gave me at the beginning of my story, when He said "All I am doing is taking away the broken petals." What made this gift extra special was that we knew the Sisters only go out of the grounds on particular occasions. They had just given me what could have been the last roses of summer. God you are truly amazing and I pray that their roses will bloom more and more every year from now on. Tears were shed as we said our goodbyes and with Sister Regina's promise that they would continue to pray for us, we set off on our journey again, this time to Dublin.

Chapter Fourteen
Bridge Over Troubled Waters

On the outskirts of Dublin, we were met by Peter Bradshaw from UCB (United Christian Broadcasters) radio. I had spoken to Peter before, when he interviewed me on the radio before leaving England. We met up with others and after a time of prayer and refreshment, we were escorted around the historical sites in Dublin, stopping at appropriate places to pray.

One of the highlights of the day for me was meeting Captain Tim Hyde, from Saint Patrick's Cathedral. Tim has written a booklet called *A Journey of Faith*. This booklet guides people around the Cathedral, as well as challenges them on issues of faith. For example, at the "Door of Reconciliation" it asks "Is Jesus waiting outside the door of your life at this time? Are you going to open the door and let Him in?" I think this booklet is brilliant and I pray that other churches will copy this idea. As the Cathedral was desecrated when Cromwell's army used it to stable their horses, it was a privilege for us to pray with Tim and bless both the Cathedral and his work there.

I had been asked to speak that evening at the celebration of the "Power to Change" campaign. Although I knew I only had a short time, I wanted to give the people a flavour of what had happened so far. When I had finished Lance, one of the team, who was carrying a burden for the rape of the ladies, stood to his feet. He choked back tears as he asked forgiveness for what the soldiers had done to the women during Cromwell's attack. "I feel so ashamed. Will you please forgive us?" he said as he sunk to the floor. I continued to read the letter, surprisingly without any tears this time. That was at least until Paddy Monaghan walked up to me and took my hand and putting his other hand on Lance's head, pronounced forgiveness on us both. It was as if the dam had burst and I instantly started to weep. The tears just kept coming and coming, I didn't seem to have any control over them. We were told later many people's lives were touched and changed. A real sign of things to come!

We stayed the next two nights outside Dublin, at Greystones Bible College. We had planned to have some time off and spent the morning walking by the sea, just allowing God to refresh our bodies as well as our spirits. That afternoon Annette was reading the newspaper and became increasingly annoyed about an article criticising the "Power to Change" campaign. "Why is it that the press just love to put Christian things down?" she said. In the end, she put the paper down, she just couldn't read any more.

The next morning at prayers, Annette told us that the previous evening when we were in the prayer room, she was praying for Ireland when she started to cry. She said she was still angry about the newspaper article, but felt God say "Don't be cross with them, Annette, pray for them, it's not their fault they don't understand." She continued, "I found that hard at first, but as I prayed, I had a vision, I saw Heaven open and a face appeared in the clouds and smiled on the land. As I watched, two big hands parted the cloud and lifted the land of Ireland and held it, as though to His chest. God said "I love this land like a father loves a child and I long to hold it close." This made me weep even more and I continued to cry for about another ten minutes. Then God said to me, "You can stop weeping now Annette and give Ireland back to me, because I love this land like its father, England, never could." This reminded me of the Family Portrait. (A word given in the nineties, in which England is represented as the father, who raped Ireland the mother and produced Northern Ireland the child.). She went on "I watched as the big hands gently lowered the island of Ireland back into the sea. A brilliant light glowed all around the island and a cross appeared in the centre." I have known Annette for a number of years now and I trust her completely. We knew this was from God.

It was lunchtime when we arrived at Wicklow and it seemed an ideal place to linger over a meal. So we went in search of a restaurant and we found the perfect place. We had just settled down to eat, when over the radio came the song "Bridge over troubled water, I will lay me down." This was the song given to me with the picture of a bridge between Ireland and England, back in March 2001. Once again, we felt God was confirming that we were on course.

On arrival in Wexford, we were met by about thirty people from a variety of churches. We shared a short service before walking over the bridge and in to town. I want to share some of the service with you, because for us it was a very moving moment:

"The Town of Wexford was assaulted in 1649 by your fore-fathers, led by Oliver Cromwell. We, in our time, being united in our decision to live in all things according to the Word of God, wish to approach the "Cromwell Event" in the spirit of forgiveness, re-pentance and reconciliation." Scriptures were read that made it clear that we all have sinned and fallen short of God's glory, and "Because God forgives our sins, we must forgive others." Then, totally unex-pected, they said they forgave Cromwell before we had had a chance to say anything. They repented for their sin of hatred, bitterness and division, as well as their thoughts, words and actions in response to Cromwell's military campaign. They declared restoration for the people of Huntingdon and Wexford and declared the bond of unity, by speaking out the scripture; "*There is one Father and one spirit just as we were called to one hope when we were called one Lord, one faith, one baptism, one God and Father of all. Now to him who is able to do immeasurable more than we can ask, think or imagine, according to His power that is at work within us, to him be glory in the church and in Christ Jesus throughout all generations, forever and ever. Amen.*" (Ephesians 4 v 4 & 3 v 20).

Walking into Wexford, we stopped by the Quay. I was pleased about this as I thought it would give us a chance to express our repentance before going any further. Because part of our commit-ment was to never impose our agenda, we waited a while. Little did we know that God had more surprises in store! A gentleman next to me started to pray with real emotion in his voice. I was surprised at what I was hearing. He was asking God to forgive him for the way he had taught history over the years, particularly Cromwell's invasion. He went on. "I know that I have taught this in a way that has encouraged bitterness and anger in young lives, and for this I am truly sorry God. And I ask the people here to forgive me too." This expression of love and repentance touched everyone. Then Lance took a step forward and stood in front of him saying, "It is us who need to say sorry to you for what we have done." The two men hugged each other. The gentleman told us afterwards that as an historian, he had been reluctant to come. However, at his church that morning, the priest had been talking about forgiveness and he had felt God challenge him. He knew he had to attend, and I was so glad he had, because I believe God wanted him free of any guilt that he carried.

Our next stop was the Franciscan Friary. It was here that seven friars had been killed by Cromwell's men in 1649 and another four in 1655. During our walk Georgina had come alongside me and said, "Shirley, I have a surprise for you. Do you remember the Guardian and Priest you met here in March?" I nodded. "Well, both men have moved on and we have two new men here now, and they are very enthusiastic about your visit and have arranged a service of reconciliation." I could hardly speak I was so amazed! There was another surprise in store as walked up to the church. There on the door was a large notice saying "Welcome Arise Ministries". After the meeting in March, we just hadn't expected this. How much more could God do to show us that He had prepared the way?

The new Guardian and the Parish Priest led a wonderful service of reconciliation. "Your coming here is an extraordinary gesture and a building of a bridge between us. Baptism unites us all and although we may be different, we are all near neighbours. The memory of Cromwell is seared on the memory of the Wexford people." He quoted Cromwell's report to the English Parliament in which he says, "We put to the sword all who came our way." He continued "Peace will depend on people's respect for each other." He prayed for those who have been maimed by sectarian violence, and as he finished speaking a spontaneous applause rang out through the church. "May the grace of God be with us to erase the memories of the past," he concluded to renewed applause.

Georgina went over to him and asked if I could speak and permission was given. I stood for a short while looking around at all the faces, and marvelling at how God had made this possible before saying "We would like to thank you for your welcome. As we arrived and saw the notice on the door, we knew that your hearts were open to us, and this has touched us deeply. In Hebrews 12 v 15b, it says *"See that no one misses the grace of God, and that no bitter root grows up to cause trouble and defile ma*ny." Then verse 24 says *"To Jesus the mediator of a new covenant, and to the sprinkled blood that speaks a better word than the blood of Abel."* This is the time for Jesus to heal the wound and cleanse it from all the blood that was shed here long ago. This can only happen through Him. It is difficult for us to put our feelings into words, but we have come here today to say we are sorry and ask the people of Wexford to forgive us, as people from Cromwell's town. I have brought with me a letter from the churches in Huntingdon and I would like to read it to you." I took a deep breath. I could feel an overwhelming sense of sadness as I began to read. Before too long, the emotion got to me and the tears started to run down my face. This was one of the hardest things I had ever had to do, it was almost as though I could feel their pain. Katie came and stood behind me. I struggled on, but it was hard to speak through the tears, and I wasn't the only one crying.

When I had finished, there was a moment of complete silence, after which the Parish Priest approached me and gave me a hug of peace. Stephen's father, Rev Frank Forbes, also stood up. He too wanted to welcome us on behalf of the Church of Ireland. He said that he was greatly moved by the spirit of this day, and went on to ask forgiveness from us for what Irish people had done to the British. We gave this willingly. I have rarely experienced such acceptance and love. Truly, God had done something amazing.

That week in the local press nearly a whole page was given over to report on the day;

"For over 750 years, Wexford Franciscan Friary has had sights of Christian affection and service, oceans of humanity and also barbarism." (Some of the history was then recounted) "Yes, there may have been sights of Christian sacrifice and joy, cruelty and controversy. But it is doubtful if a more astounding and pleasant scene was ever witnessed like the one on last Sunday afternoon. Members of a Christian Prayer group of several denominations came from the birthplace of Oliver Cromwell to the Friary to apologise to the people of Wexford for the cruelties and deaths inflicted in October 1649. An apology and an exchange of remorse and love after three hundred and fifty years is indeed amazing. But it was inspired in the prayer group by a compulsion to share Christian kindness in the heart-warming effort for reconciliation." After reporting almost every detail of the service, the article concluded by saying. "The request for a sign of peace by Shirley Bowers was obeyed with moving intensity. The group mingled with the congregation amid mutual welcoming and greetings as warm as any Christmas family reunion. We left feeling, I would say, elevated in spirit."

(Reporter; Nicky Furlong).

The service at Pat Murphy's church that evening was more informal and gave people a chance to share their feelings. One lady told us how she had been praying for years for someone to deal with this issue of Cromwell. Annette shared her vision from the day before, and a lady in the congregation testified how that morning she had prayed that God would hold Ireland like a baby. It was a day to remember!

The next day began with an amazing time of prayer. We felt as if God was pouring more blessing onto us, so much so that we almost couldn't take it all. After breakfast, we headed off into the town. Georgina was at work, but Stephen was free to escort us. During the Civil War, the streets of Wexford were reported to be like rivers of blood. So, we decided to share Holy Communion, remembering that Jesus died to bring forgiveness and reconciliation to a broken world. So, carrying the wine and bread rolls, we set off. Stephen and I were walking along chatting together, when suddenly, I looked down and there in the gutter, lay two whole fish! I was reminded of the picture given to me of Jesus placing in my hands loaves and fishes (you can read this story in chapter nine). We had the bread with us and now here were the fish. "How often do you see fish in the street?" I asked Stephen, "Never," he replied. I felt Jesus was reminding me that all we have to do is offer the little bit we have to Him, and then watch what He can do.

Pat Murphy joined us and over lunch, he told us that we had been invited to a village not far from Wexford, called Courtna-cuddy. The Priest there, he told us, had prayed for reconciliation for twenty eight years and eight of them specifically about the Cromwell issue. This is another example of our being there as a result of other people's prayer.

As we arrived at the church, we were welcomed by the Priest, Father Finn, and escorted to the front of the church. I was invited to take my place on one side of the altar and Father Finn on the other. After introductions he said "We are standing here with over 350 years of history. However, it only takes a small number with a pro-phetic vision to create a climate of change and bring forth the word of God into every situation. This has been prayed for by us here and by those in Huntingdon for many years, and now is the time for change to take place."

I was asked to respond to this by sharing my testimony in which I included the story of the rose. I felt uncomfortable being so far away from Father Finn, so I asked if I could cross over to where he was. As I stood next to him, the words of remorse and tears came pouring out. I remember the burden seemed almost too much to bear and I became bent over with the pain. Father Finn just gently put his arm around me and laid his other hand on my head. We stayed like this for a little while before he pronounced forgiveness in an extremely loving way. He said "We are so grateful that you have made this journey. I heard of your coming through Pat Murphy. When we knew that the group was going to Wexford, I thought it would be good for you to come here to Courtnacuddy. I knew this was right when Shirley shared the story of the rose. Before you came, we thought it would be good to mark this occasion by asking you to plant a rose tree in our garden here." I smiled, once again not being able to believe what I was hearing. He went on "When the rose tree was bought, it had only one red rose on it. We take that as a sign from God that what has taken place here tonight is good and right, and with the assurance that not only did He plan this, but He is mighty." Continuing he said, "Shirley, please go back to Huntingdon and tell our brothers and sisters there that Christ's blood has washed away our sins and reconciled us. Christ has broken down the wall that has been a source of division between our people for hundreds of years. I pray that the fruit of our gathering here tonight may bear fruit for generations to come. The Bible says "*How blessed are they that bring good news, announcing glad tidings, peace and reconciliation.*" Tonight, you have come and brought reconciliation for hundreds of years of history. Tell that to your people when you go back."

Handing the framed letter to Father Finn I said, "Our prayer is that many people will be able to read this and find hope and healing." He presented us with a banner which, he told us, the diocese had designed especially for the millennium. I couldn't take my eyes off the words written at the bottom. It read "FROM HISTORY TO HOPE". He passed it to me saying, "Your presence here, I believe, is an answer to this prayer of ours over two years ago. Thank you again for coming." There were no words I could say that would be adequate. I felt overwhelmed.

The time had flown by and it was getting dark outside. Car

headlights lit the garden so we could see to plant the rose. Earlier, when they had been preparing the ground, they had dug out seven large stones from the hole. They took this as yet another sign from God, as there were seven of us, and we each took a turn in planting the rose tree. Once again I read the scripture, "*Pass through the gates. Remove the stones. Prepare the way for the people.*" Everyone joined in at the end with a loud "Amen!"

It was about nine o'clock now and we thought that the evening was at an end. However, we were pleasantly surprised to be invited to join them at their weekly prayer meeting. The presence of God was tangible that night as we worshipped Him together. The Holy Spirit came in power as we prayed for each person and anointed them with oil. One lady told us that she had been in Ireland for eighteen years and for all this time, she had been ashamed to say she was English, because of the way the English had treated the Irish. "But tonight," she said "Jesus has healed me!" We were ready to leave Wexford now, knowing what God had planned, He had also accomplished.

We arrived on the outskirts of Waterford the next afternoon. As we crossed over the bridge that leads into the city, we were told that it was from here that many young men had committed suicide. "Sadly," I said "this seems to be a recurring theme wherever we go." I was reminded how many Irish Catholics were drowned as they were driven off their land. I also remembered that in Huntingdon we too had suffered quite a few suicides, as well as accidental deaths, of young people drowning in our river. Have we reaped what Cromwell had sown?

I remember praying about this in Huntingdon years ago and the feeling of anger I had towards Satan. How dare he rob these young people of their lives! As we stood on the bridge, I asked God to forgive the sins of the past, and heal the broken-hearted. There was a real sense of God's presence. I told Satan that he was not going to claim any more lives by bringing his destruction and death because Jesus is more powerful and "He who is in us is greater than he that is in the world" (1 John 4 v 4). I poured oil into the river as a sign of healing. The bridge is one of the main roads linking Huntingdon to the busy A14 road, yet while we were there, not a single vehicle crossed, not even a bicycle. However, as we prayed, the bridge physically shook. Not just slightly, it really shook. We all looked at each other in disbelief, not knowing if we had imagined it, but we all felt it and knew that God had done something. It was an awesome experience.

Now in Waterford we were hearing the same story. So, we prayed and watched as the oil was poured into the water, where it formed a perfect rainbow, "God's promise" we said. We were told when we returned to England, that the suicide rate had dropped dramatically. Praise you Lord!

Due to an oversight in the bookings for the evening celebration, two speakers had been arranged. As I was second, when I got up to speak I asked the Pastor how long I had. I remember him replying with a smile "Until midnight!" That straight away took any pressure off me and I was able to relax and give my testimony, as well as present the letter. When I had finished, a grey-haired lady in front of me leaned back in her chair saying "That has blown my mind. I believe there will be a revival here!" I thought to myself even if nothing else happens here tonight, it was worth coming just for her.

We hadn't been told of any of the problems before we arrived, so what happened next came as quite a shock. The Pastor rose and stood in front of everyone, saying he had a confession to make. I wondered what this was about. He continued to say that before we came, he didn't believe that what we were doing was of God. He even confessed later to Annette that when he heard the "a net" part of the story, he and others had laughed in disbelief. "However," he went on, "after hearing your testimony tonight, I know I was wrong. So I am asking you, Shirley and all of you from Huntingdon and also from Waterford, to please forgive me!" He said with sincerity, "I am so sorry. I am so sorry!" This took great humility and courage and I had no problem releasing him of any guilt he may have felt. He later asked if we would be kind enough to accept the evening's offering, saying "I pray this will help you a little on your journey." It certainly did, but it wasn't the money that helped, it was the spirit in which it had been given. Waterford what you have sown, you will also reap.

We were prayer walking around the city the next day when I felt a nudge to buy a key. At the time, I had no idea why, but later I remembered the bunch of keys given to me back in 1999. The shopkeeper told us that the key we had chosen was an old jailer's key. One of the scriptures for Waterford was from Luke 4 v 18, when Jesus said *"He has sent me to proclaim freedom for the prisoners."* We believed this word was also for one of the ladies with us and we gave her the key. When a family have been dispossessed of their land as hers had, and the pattern keeps being repeated, it can feel as though you are in a prison. God wanted her to know she had been given the key as a sign that this was a new day, because He was in the process of setting her city and her family free.

With our time here at an end, we were again ready to move on to Cork.

Chapter Fifteen
Giving Back the City

Driving along the quayside into Cork, we saw a car sitting by the side of the road with a huge sign on the windscreen saying "ARISE! WELCOME". As we pulled over, I once again felt the nudge from the Holy Spirit to buy a key. How can we do this? I knew we were going straight into the city centre to meet Sister Bridget. I went over to Annette in the other car, and told her what I was thinking. "The Bible says that if two agree then it shall be done. So, can we agree together that when we get into the city centre, there will be a place to buy a key." "Certainly" she replied. We drove into the car park and went down in the lift. The lift doors opened and right in front of us was, yes you've guessed it, a kiosk selling keys!

After lunch, we prayer walked around the old city wall. Cork was once surrounded by water and therefore hard to defeat. We were told that Cork had only surrendered to Cromwell because a local man opened the gates while the city slept. As we stood in one of the oldest streets, we asked God for His forgiveness for the pain that had been caused by this act of betrayal and the subsequent surrender. I knew now why I had to give them the key. I felt that it was as if I was giving them back their city. Everyone laughed as I handed it over. Apparently, Sister Bridget had been given a key ring a while ago and God had told her to wait for the key! Wow!

God hadn't finished with us as we discovered when we gathered together the following morning for prayer and Holy Communion. One of the ladies had a picture; it was of a rose with its stem sharpened to a point. The rose was thrown and hit the centre of a dart board. She felt God was saying to us that we were right on target.

We left Cork knowing that God had met with His people. Here,

as elsewhere where we were unable to meet Catholic or City officials, we made sure that they didn't miss out on the blessing, by
delivering the letter to the Bishop's residence and the City Hall.

By now, word about our journey had spread and we were asked to
visit Callan, a small town not far from Kilkenny. When we arrived,
we were met by a number of people at Skerry's Castle. Part of the old
wall that defended the town against Cromwell's attack still exists.
Among the people present were several historians, including their
spokesperson, Philip Lynch and two Councillors. The welcome we
received once again was full of kindness and good wishes. A couple
from Laois told me later that they had travelled quite a distance after
hearing about our journey on the radio. "It was important for us to
meet you personally. That's how much your visit means to us here in
Ireland!" they said. Although we are conscious that this land was
deeply wounded, we were amazed that our journey was having such a
profound impact on the people.

This is a quote from the local newspaper, Kilkenny People:
"We're sorry for the pain he caused you. What he did was wrong
and we are here to apologise." That was the message to the people of
Callan from a group representing seven churches in Huntingdon,
the Cambridgeshire town that gave birth to Cromwell. The group,
made up of Christians from all denominations, were in Ireland on a
mission of peace and reconciliation. Popular local historian, Philip
Lynch, greeted Shirley Bowers, leader of the Huntingdon group and
her colleagues. "You come on a different mission to that of Huntingdon's most noted citizen," he intoned "and we appreciate that.
He came to wreck, to tear down and to destroy our little town. It
took Callan over a hundred years to recover." Mr Lynch made the
point that the visitors' kindly gesture could be seen as yet another
reminder that God triumphs in the end and that if people obeyed
the commandment to love one another, there would be no more
wars." Councillors Tommy Maher and Jimmy Brett both praised
what Councillor Brett described as the group's "courageous act". As

I take time now to recall that day, although it was unplanned and informal, it was one of the special moments in our memories of Ireland.

With this visit behind us, we now had to focus on our next destination Kilkenny. We had been asked to take part in a radio broadcast with Father Dan Carroll. I started to think back on how many times in the past I had been afraid of speaking to anyone, even to friends. God reminded me of all He had done to bring this healing. Now, here I am in Ireland meeting civic dignitaries, clergy, and people I have never met before, as well as recording radio broadcasts. I was reminded of a scripture that had been spoken over me, way back in the Eighties. It was from Jeremiah 1 v 6-9; *"Ah, Sovereign Lord," I said, "I do not know how to speak, I am only a child."* (Or in my case shy and afraid like a child.) *"But the Lord said to me, Do not say, I am only a child. You must go to everyone I send you to and say whatever I command you. Do not be afraid of them, for I am with you and will rescue you," declares the Lord. Then the Lord reached out his hand and touched my mouth and said to me. "Now, I have put my words in your mouth."*

When we arrived, we were shown into the reception room, where Father Carroll joined us. He was a big man with an equally big personality. I felt the pressure taken off me straight away when he asked Phyllis from Omagh, if she would take part in the broadcast too. Phyllis came over really well. She shared her delight in being part of this trip, and how she believed that it would bring healing to this land she loved so much, North and South. Even though many lost their lives when her hometown was bombed in 1998, she holds no malice and thanked everyone for their prayers. Afterwards I shared about our trip, and Father Carroll asked the final question. "So Shirley, where to next?" I replied saying that we would be travelling up to Athlone, where the Catholic people were herded across the bridges into the West. Cromwell is alleged to have said, "To Hell or Connaught." I went on, "I don't know if that is true or not, but anyway, we feel we should cross over into Con-

naught too. Where we will be going after that, we haven't a clue."
"Neither had they!" Father Carroll answered rather appropriately!

The following day we woke again to brilliant sunshine. We had been told that the plan for the day was to meet the Mayor on the outskirts of Kilkenny, and then be taken to a civic reception, as well as a service in the Cathedral. This could have been another nerve-racking experience for me, but God was teaching me step by step that I was to put my whole trust in Him and not be afraid. As well as meeting the dignitaries, I was surprised to see Philip Lynch again. We had only met the previous day in Callan, but he told us he was so touched by what we were doing that he wanted to be part of this day too! After the official photographs, we set off on what the news-paper described as "a peace walk" to the City Hall. As the Mayor and I walked together, she struck me as a very gracious lady, with a real sense of justice and truth.

We arrived at City Hall and while we were having refreshments, Annette was once again on the hunt for keys. We had come to realise that the picture of a bunch of keys God had given me in Carrickfergus in 1999 was for giving back the land to the people of Ireland. If only I had realised that earlier, I would have saved Ann-ette a lot of trouble! The Mayor welcomed us and spoke enthusias-tically of the city, both its history and the present. Concluding she said, "Once again you are very welcome here and I appreciate the spirit in which you have come." I was moved to hear her express herself in this way. I knew without a doubt God had gone ahead of us as He promised He would. So without hesitation I was able to share how I believed it was God's desire to bring His healing and reconciliation to this part of history, before reading and presenting her with the letter. I then took the key, and before placing it into her hand, I asked her to forgive the part that Cromwell played in their history. "Lady Mayor, this is a spiritual thing we are doing here today. So I would like you to accept this key as a symbol of freedom and the handing back of Kilkenny to you as its leading citizen." I was in tears and as I looked around, I could see others were too.

They all clapped enthusiastically. What a privilege it is to do this work for God and see the difference it was making to people's lives!

Afterwards, we were led through the streets of Kilkenny by Rev Stephen Taylor, the Methodist minister and onto St Canice's Cathedral. Here we were welcomed by the Dean, a Catholic Priest representing the Bishop, and Father Carroll, who we had met the day before, representing St Patrick's Parish. To our astonishment, the Cathedral was closed to the public so that a service could be held in our honour. This took a very informal stance as everyone, including the clergy, was invited to share what was on their heart. The Dean concluded this time with a short address. After I had spoken and presented the letter, I asked all the clergy if they would mind joining me at the front. I took their hands and joining them together, placed a key in the centre and told them, "God has given you the key to unity. If there was one lesson to be learned from Cromwell it's this, never allow religion to get in the way of Christianity. That which once brought division between us, can now be used to bring unity to the body of Christ, just as our Saviour prayed in John 17 "*that the world may see.*"

We had a long drive ahead of us to Athlone, in the centre of Ireland. We drove a different route to the one we took in March. This time, we passed miles and miles of black land where the peat had been extracted. As I looked across the fields, I couldn't help but compare this barren land with what had happened all those years ago. Cromwell thought that what he was doing was the will of God, but instead what he was sowing was to keep this land and its people in bondage and pain for centuries.

On reaching Athlone, we had arranged to meet and pray on the bridge in the town before the evening service. We were astonished at how many turned up. I don't know if Cromwell ever did say "To Hell or Connaught" or even if this bridge existed in1649, but that's not important. What we do know is that many Catholic people died as a result of being herded across the rivers to the West, and many of those who managed to survive died later of starvation. This bridge in Athlone represented all the others, so it was decided that as part of our prayer, we would do a prophetic act. I asked all who were Catholic, or who identified themselves with the Catholics, to go to the western side of the bridge while everyone else stayed on the other. Both sides would then walk across, meet in the middle and welcome - the opposite of how the people were treated years ago. As we did this there was an eerie silence. Nobody seemed to want to talk. As we drew closer together, the excitement grew. The experience was more emotional than I had expected, and many people, including me, were in tears as we met and embraced each other. At that moment, the sky grew menacing and dark and it looked as if we were going to be caught in a storm. Next, something surreal happened - a funeral procession crossed over the bridge. It was a Sunday evening and I had never seen this before. It was as if God was saying, "This is the death of the old order of things." Then, just as suddenly, the sky became lighter and a flock of birds flew overhead, as if God was saying there is a new freedom here now. Many of those who were on the Catholic side told me later that they had never experienced anything like this, they just felt so accepted and loved.

At the evening service, I introduced each member of the team and encouraged them to share how they had come to be on this journey. After I shared my testimony, a Catholic Priest came to the front. I felt myself becoming emotional again as I asked him and the Catholic people for forgiveness, before reading the letter. Surprisingly, it was the men that God touched that night as their tears flowed freely. After a while, a gentleman came forward, asking forgiveness for the Irish people's attitude towards the English. This meant so much to us. A Catholic lady spoke a prophetic word and told us later, that she had never done this before. She believed that because that day she felt so accepted and loved, God had healed her and released her from the fear she had of speaking out.

The following morning, we attended the service at the Catholic Church where I had been asked to speak. The church was huge, almost like a Cathedral and I felt strange as I took the long walk to the front, passing the coffin we had seen the previous evening. The Priest encouraged me to share what was on my heart, which I did before reading the letter and presenting it to the church. After the service, many of the congregation came to talk and ask for prayer. Some were suffering with cancer, others depression, many with tears as they accepted God's love for them. We also prayed with men who had previously been involved in the IRA movement. They were asking for forgiveness for those who had been killed and maimed over the years. Leaving these people in God's hands, we left that day in awe of God.

We spent the next two days travelling around the West of Ireland, leaving the letter with an explanation where we could, occasionally with the Priest and if not, in the church. We met some very interesting people during this time and we knew God was in it all, even the Bed and Breakfast where we stayed. The owner had no knowledge of what we were doing when he shared with us that he could trace his family right back to Cromwell's time, and that they were some of the first people to be driven over into Connaught. This was no coincidence. Before we left, we prayed a blessing over this family. We declared that they would prosper above and beyond anything they could have even imagined. The curse was reversed!

We were now heading back to Northern Ireland, to "Crossfire Trust" near Crossmaglen on the border. It was good to have this time to unwind before heading home. After breakfast the following morning, we met together in the prayer room. While we were worshipping, I noticed some flags curled up in the corner. I went over and picked one up. As I unfurled it, I couldn't believe what I saw. I held it high, and everyone in the room seemed to gasp at the same time. On it was a map of Ireland, with light shining all around the land and a cross in the centre, with the words "It is finished" at the top. "That is it - that is the picture I saw at Greystones!" Annette cried. What more could God do to show us that this was His plan and that the cross and the blood that Jesus shed that day long ago can bring reconciliation and healing. I am sure the angels must have been singing with us that day as we worshipped God. The whole room seemed to vibrate with praise!

Later as we prayed with people in their shop, a lady put a cross and chain around my neck. "God told me I was to give this to you," she said "to show our unity." That was the final blessing! It also reminds me of what Jesus said in John 17 v 23 *May they be brought to complete unity to let the world know that you sent me and have loved them, even as you have loved me.*" I believe that is what our journey was all about - letting the people know that God loves them and cares about their pain.

We had all taken this trip in faith, both for our provision and not knowing what God had in store for us. We travelled with only enough money for the first two nights' accommodation, the rest we were going to put on a credit card. However, God was so faithful to us and the people of Ireland were so hospitable and generous. We arrived back in England with just the right amount of money to fill the cars up with petrol to get us home. This meant we finished our journey without any outstanding bills!

I had no idea when we set out on this venture whether the people of Ireland would understand and welcome us, or just see me as an eccentric lady with a crazy idea. My heart's desire was for God to bring His healing to this land and that nobody would miss His love and blessing. The people of Ireland proved that any fears I may have had were unfounded. Never in all my life have I experienced anything like those few weeks. It had been a real privilege and very humbling to serve the Irish people in this way and I know I speak for the whole team. Whether it was the people in the streets we met, Deans, Mayors, Priests or Nuns, it made no difference. They all opened not only their arms to us, but their hearts also.

Thank you Ireland, your memory will live in our hearts forever!

Chapter Sixteen
You Reap What You Sow

It was so good to be home again. However, Tony's throat problem was ongoing and still concerned me. His tonsil was very large and following another visit to the doctor, he was referred to an ear, nose and throat specialist. We were told the tonsil needed to be removed and sent away for examination and this operation was done almost straight away. The time of waiting was hard, but I think both of us knew what the result would be. Unfortunately, it turned out to be a cancerous growth and the beginning of six weeks of daily radiotherapy treatments for Tony.

During this time, we were surrounded with the love and prayers of so many people and I know that this made all the difference. However, it was still very hard for all the family as we watched him suffer. His mouth became red raw inside and his tongue was swollen, which made eating almost impossible. As a result, he lost over three and a half stone and he looked as if he was dying. In fact, Tony himself believed he was and we all prepared ourselves. Despite all of this, we had a real sense of God's peace. Apart from our faith, we believed this peace was the result of an experience Tony had about thirty years earlier. It happened one night soon after we had gone to bed. We were just laying there, talking over the day's events, when suddenly Tony fell silent. Although this was unusual, I didn't think anything of it at the time. I just thought he had fallen asleep. A few minutes later, he was making a strange noise, so I shook him. "What a weird experience!" he said before turning over and going to sleep.

It wasn't until the following morning that I was to find out what had happened. He explained that as we were talking together, he found himself tingling from head to foot "as if I was going under an anaesthetic," he said. "Then suddenly, I was in a place where the light was so brilliant and the joy indescribable." He went on. "I didn't feel any fear, just pure joy and happiness. It was as if all the prayers I have ever prayed had been answered." Then just as suddenly, he had felt a pain in his chest. He tried to move his arm, but it wouldn't move. He tried to call my name and I expect that was the noise I heard, and then he was back with me. He said, "Do you know Shirley, I will never, ever be afraid of dying. The love, peace and joy I felt there was beyond words." I can honestly say I stopped worrying about Tony's future at that point because I knew God had shown me that He had him in His hands. So we believed beyond doubt, as we faced this cancer together, that all would be well. No matter what the future held for us, we trusted God. People who visited our home spoke of the peace they felt there and I know this was a real witness to God's amazing love and power. When Jesus said "*I will never leave you or forsake you*," He really meant it!

One morning about two thirds of the way through his treatment, I couldn't stand seeing him in so much pain any longer. I prayed that if the treatment was going to cure him that God would get him through it, no matter how hard that was going to be. However, if it wasn't going to cure him, that God would stop it. Although I had prayed for his healing many times, somehow today's prayer was different, this time it was unconditional as I surrendered all to God. That evening, Tony, with no knowledge of my prayer, told me he had decided to stop the treatment. When I asked him why, he told me that he had asked God to help him, because he knew he had come to the end and couldn't go on any longer. "As I lay in the bath," he went on, "a drop of water fell from the shower right onto my head and instantly I was filled with peace, and I knew I had made the right decision."

The following day, we returned to the hospital and asked to speak to the consultant. They did everything they could to try and persuade him to change his mind. They even told us that the cancer could return very quickly and his decision to stop the treatment could be fatal. "No," he said firmly, "I have made up my mind, I am going to trust God." This was hard for the family, but they also knew that he couldn't go on suffering in the way he had been. I would be lying if I said that the weeks that followed were easy, because they weren't. During this time though, God's peace never left us. It took quite a while for Tony to begin to recover and start eating properly again. However, we all knew he had made the right decision. That is now many years ago, and praise God the cancer hasn't returned!

I believe that once again, we were reaping what we had sown. You may remember at the beginning of the book I told you how I felt God had shown me that Cromwell's actions were like a cancer which had spread out and affected many parts of this land, including Ireland. The Brazilian Pastor in 1999 said that he believed that Cromwell made Ireland sick. Well, I believe that our trip to Ireland had began a healing process and just like the cancer in Tony's throat, by the power of God, this cancer would also be healed. It is well known that unforgiveness causes bitterness and this can block our spiritual growth, as well as our physical healing. I believe God has touched many lives and worked miracles that we may never know about. He is Almighty God, and unbelievable as it may seem, He chooses to use people like you and me. In James 1 v 2, it says *"Consider it pure joy, my brothers, whenever you face trials of many kinds because you know that the testing of your faith develops perseverance."* Well, we had been well and truly tested, not only in the last few months but over the years. However, through it all, God has been refining us, chipping away the rough edges and making us more like Him. He still has a lot to do but, by His grace, He will finish what He has begun.

Many people over the years had suggested that I should write a book about my experiences, but I have to say for someone who hates putting pen to paper, this seemed like a bad joke! However as time went by the idea grew on me. One evening as I was sharing this with Vanessa she surprised me by saying that she had been trained as an editor. I was so shocked, I couldn't believe my ears! She continued, "I really think this story should be told and I would love to help, but my training is as an editor, I am not a writer."

On another occasion, I received a package from Ireland. It was a book that a friend had written in which she mentioned our visit. This started me thinking again about writing my own story. However, this thought didn't last long, because I still believed God would provide me with a "ghost writer". I was more than happy to wait and see what happened next!

I didn't have to wait long as one Sunday morning, a gentleman turned up at church who was very interested in our recent trip to Ireland. As we talked together he told me his wife was thought to be related in some way to Cromwell. I was taken aback. I foolishly told him I was thinking of writing a book and he seemed really interested. He surprised me by saying, "Please keep in touch as I would like to help finance this." OK God, I get the hint!

However, the days that followed seemed to fly by and I soon forgot all about writing. I had other things on my mind. It was now early in the year 2003, and I received a telephone call telling me that the Mayor of Drogheda, Malachy Godfrey and his brother Frank, a former Mayor, had expressed a desire to visit Huntingdon. This was more than we could have even imagined and we wanted to make it a memorable occasion.

The next few weeks were to be a bit hectic. We sent out invitations, booked a hall for a reception, and made plans for the day. We decided that as this was about building bridges between our communities, we would like to entertain our guests for lunch at the "Old Bridge Hotel." So Vanessa and I made arrangements to see someone there. We didn't feel it was appropriate to share all that this visit represented, but we did tell the booking manager that we were expecting dignitaries from Ireland. "That sounds interesting," she replied, and offered us one of their rooms free of charge. "Would you like to see it now?" she said. She escorted us down a short corridor. "We call this the Cromwell Room" she said as we went through the door. Well, you could have knocked us down with a feather. We hadn't mentioned Cromwell at all. Yet another confirmation!

Soon the day of the reception arrived and the Huntingdon Mayor and Mayoress, Cllrs Jeff and Claire Dutton and his Deputy were among the first to arrive. I find it hard to explain how I felt seeing the dignitaries from Huntingdon and Drogheda standing side by side, worshipping God as we sang the first hymn. I read a letter from Jonathan Djanogly, the Member of Parliament for Huntingdon. It read that he really wanted to be with us, but he was otherwise engaged. He continued, "I would be most grateful if you could extend my welcome and apologies for absence to all our visitors from Ireland." As Cromwell was once the leader of Parliament, I felt this welcome was very important for our guests from Ireland to hear.

I shared some thoughts on how we as Christians are given the ministry of reconciliation, quoting 2 Corinthians 5 v 18; "*All this is from God, who reconciled us to himself through Christ and gave to us the ministry of reconciliation.*" I went on, "I believe God wants to build a bridge between our communities, so that those who once were enemies, can now be friends. I believe this is what all this is about, God reaching down through history and healing the division." Malachy's reply couldn't have been better if I had written it myself. He said "My brother and I have come here today to offer the hand of friendship to this your town of Huntingdon."

I thought it couldn't get any better than this. Then Jeff, the Mayor of Huntingdon rose to reply, "Some things in history we are proud of and some we are not. Today, we are writing tomorrow's history." As the two Mayors stood side by side, I couldn't help but think how only a few months ago this would never have been possible. God had worked a miracle! I remembered that when we visited Drogheda the prayer group there prayed with Malachy, and I knew that Jeff and his wife were both Christians, so I did something that I hadn't planned on doing. I asked them if they would mind me praying for them. They agreed. I reached out and took hold of both men's hands, joining them together. As I did this, something inside of me broke. Many years ago God asked me "Will you stand in the gap?" This day, I felt honoured to be standing between these two leaders. It felt as if here and now part of the gap had been bridged. The former town clerk of Huntingdon added to this later when he said in his address, "This day, we are turning a new page in history." Everyone applauded. What a morning!

After our guests had returned to Ireland, life seemed a little quiet. However, just as Malachy had promised, it wasn't long before I received a telephone call from the new Mayor of Drogheda, Cllr Maria O'Brien Campbell. She invited us for an official visit once again on September 11th and hoped the Mayor of Huntingdon would come too. I was thrilled and after speaking to Jeff, our Mayor, he was just as delighted and he and Claire accepted the invitation without hesitation.

With only a few weeks to go, I was shocked to discover that Jeff had been admitted to hospital and needed an operation. The days flew by and the date for our visit drew closer but poor Jeff didn't seem to improve. When the hospital told him that under no circumstances was he to fly, we all knew that he wouldn't be able to join us. We were very disappointed. However, I shall never forget how, when I telephoned him to assure him of our prayers, he told me that Claire still intended to come and his Deputy, Susan Mulcahy, would be travelling in his place. I was overjoyed and very relieved!

It was September 11th and I woke feeling a little apprehensive. "Dear God," I prayed, "please help me today to say things that bring healing, the things that will build on what you have already done. Help me Father in whatever you call me to do, that I may be obedient. May everything today be done in love and to Your glory."

As we arrived at the Town Hall in Drogheda, we were shown

into the packed reception room. I was told that Tom Reilly, the gentleman who had opposed our visit last year, was also there. The Mayor, speaking with real sincerity in her voice, welcomed us all to Drogheda. She said that over dinner the previous evening she, and the Deputy Mayor and Mayoress of Huntingdon had had a very profitable discussion on ways in which the friendship that had been started last year by Arise Ministries could now be strengthened.

As Jeff had been unable to attend, Claire read a letter on his behalf, in which he expressed his regret at not being with them and sent his good wishes to the people of Drogheda. I have to say I felt honoured to be there that day with both Susan and Claire. They were a real credit to our town.

Then, it was my turn. I thanked the Mayor for her kind words, "We have for too long been enemies, it is time now for us to be friends." I went on to say how for two people in the room, this was particularly appropriate. Everyone knew without saying names who I was talking about, as Frank and Tom had been fighting in the press over Cromwell's legacy for years. "Our journey brought us here because God wants to heal the wounds from the past, so that we can put history back in its place, behind us, and treat it as such. Then we can grow in unity. This can only happen if we accept our responsibilities and start to teach history in a way that doesn't prolong the anger and bitterness. It's time we started to think of how we can build a true and worthwhile relationship." I had a real sense this was to be a turning point. I read again the churches' letter and presented it to the Mayor.

With these formalities over, I began to relax. I wasn't sure which of the gentlemen in the room was Tom Reilly until, to my surprise, he came and introduced himself. Shaking my hand, he told me he was touched by what I had said, and he agreed with me. I certainly hadn't expected that! Then to my delight, I saw him and Frank shaking hands too. The picture was later printed in the newspaper!

We spent the rest of the day sightseeing together, ending up at the Heritage Centre, with a talk by Tom Reilly. He told me afterwards that as an extra source of income, they had gone into publishing. He turned and looked me in the face and said "If you have a book in there Shirley, I could publish it for you!" Yet another prompt to get writing!

Just as we were about to leave, Frank and Malachy suddenly appeared again. I had wondered where they had gone. Frank had spoken before about getting a plaque made so that there would be a record of the Arise visit in 2002. He and Malachy reached into the boot of their car and lifted out a large marble stone. He said that he wanted our visit to be recognised so that future generations would know we were sorry for the pain caused by Cromwell and had come to Drogheda to apologise. He had done this by himself, but not everyone was happy. I believe that God is in the business of reconciling the past and maybe one day this plaque will be displayed so that many might know and be healed.

We revisited the Monastery where we had stayed the year before and Sister Regina once again shared how much it had meant to her and her fellow sisters. "We have waited a long time for this healing to happen," she said, "so after refreshment, would you mind if we all prayed together?" There was a real sense of God's presence in the room that day and we felt honoured to spend time with such gracious and gentle people. Just as we were about to leave, Sister Regina reached down and taking a rose out of the vase, she passed it to me saying, "This is from the Lord." What a blessing!

The following day, Stephen Forbes arrived to drive us down to Wexford. He told us that Pastor Pat Murphy's mother had just died and that there was to be a removal service that evening. He explained that in Ireland when someone dies, the body is taken to the church before the funeral. This is so friends can come and pay their respects and show their support for the family. We all agreed that we would like to do this too.

The church was full to capacity. It was a beautiful building and as we sat before the service, peacefully listening to the music you couldn't help but feel the presence of God. Annette told me later that she heard God speak to her during this time, saying that she was to never forget all that He had done in the last few days, and that He was going to send us to even more diverse situations. Then, loud and clear, she heard Him say, "Don't forget, Annette, you heard me here, in the Catholic Church."

The following morning Georgina and Stephen had arranged a visit to a place called Tomhaggard, a small community right in the heart of the countryside in County Wexford. We met Father Danny there, and he took us to the old graveyard, where the ruins of the medieval church were just visible. He told us their story of fear and death. He pointed over the fields, "Can you see the white rock over there? Well, that is known as a Mass rock." Back in the days of Cromwell, all the churches were desecrated and Catholic people were unable to hold Mass. So they took one of the stones from the ruined church into the forest, and this is where they held their service in secret, with watchmen up in the trees looking out for Cromwellian soldiers. He went on to tell us the priest then was Father Nicholas Mayler.

The story goes that Father Mayler asked his people that if ever he was caught, not to let his chalice fall into Cromwellian hands, but to hide it. One bleak Christmas morning in 1653, Cromwell's men caught them celebrating Mass and Father Mayler was killed on the spot. One of the ladies recovered the chalice and hid it, first in her apron and then in the reeds, from where she retrieved it later. She returned it to the Mayler family, who kept it for 236 years. One of Father Mayler's family, Archdeacon Phillip Mayler, returned it to the church in Tomhaggard in the nineteenth century. "It is, of course, very precious so it is kept safe at the bank and brought out only on special occasions, such as Mass on Christmas Day" he said. He fumbled about in his coat and to our surprise, he pulled out the chalice! It was in two pieces and after screwing them together, he placed it on the palm of my hand. The only way I can even begin to describe what happened next is by saying that the moment the chalice touched me it felt as if history and the present had come together. Years ago, this chalice was kept from Cromwellian hands and here it was being placed in mine, the person standing in the gap for Cromwell. It was very moving! Father Danny asked if we would return that evening and share our story with the folk there. I jumped at the chance. It seemed only a small thing to do for this community. He said "I'll do my best to get people here, but because it's Saturday, there might only be a few."

We set off to visit our friends in Courtnacuddy and water the rose we planted. When we arrived, we were saddened to hear we wouldn't be seeing Father Finn this time as he had moved to another parish. However, we were pleased to meet the new Priest and some familiar faces from last year. As we started to reminisce, the Priest looked puzzled, he hadn't a clue what all this was about. As I shared the story with him, you could see that he was really touched. "I have never heard of anything like this," he said "I have never come across a more Christian movement and I would like it if we could pray together before we have tea. Perhaps afterwards you may like to see our Mass rock. It is quite a walk, but it is easy to get to." We had been disappointed earlier when Father Danny had asked us the same question at Tomhaggard, but because their Mass rock was across the fields and we didn't have appropriate footwear, we had been unable to go.

Quite a crowd had gathered at the rock by the time we arrived. We were amazed at the size of it and wondered how the people long ago managed to move it to this remote spot. They must have been very determined. During a time of prayer, I confessed again the sins of the past and asked God's forgiveness for the humiliation that the people had suffered by having to hide away to worship Him. Next, just as Jacob had done in Genesis 28 v 18, we anointed the Mass rock and the Priest with oil as we blessed him and this congregation.

We had to get back for the service at Tomhaggard. We were amazed when we arrived to see the church packed. The whole village must have been there! Father Danny welcomed us and explained about our visit. I recounted last year's visit and the story behind it, before continuing onto the events of our morning there. I tried as best I could to explain how I felt when the chalice was placed on my hand, but it was difficult, and all I could say was 'sorry'. I went on, "I have been told that this is a special year for you, as it is 350 years since Father Mayler was killed. God's timing is always perfect and there couldn't be a better time to say sorry." My hands shook and tears filled my eyes as I read the letter. The room sat quiet for a second or two, and then a thunderous applause rang out. Father Danny stood to his feet. "Sure we forgive you, Shirley," he said "and you will always be welcome here, in fact we insist you return. And tonight I have a surprise for you." He leaned forward and revealed the Mayler chalice. "This is only used for special occasions and tonight is very special. So we will be using this as we share the wine together." This we knew was a huge honour. Father Danny was a real character, someone we will remember. So, we left with the promise that the letter would be put on the wall for others to read.

The following day, we were to meet the Mayor of Wexford, at the morning service at Pat Murphy's church. I felt honoured to do this as the previous year he wasn't available and I have always felt it important to speak with the Civic as well as the Church authorities. To be honest, I can't remember much of what I said that day. God just seemed to put the words in my mouth. However, I do remember feeling very moved as I spoke again of the suffering that the people had endured and of God's grace and mercy as He heals these wounds. I asked the Mayor to join me as I asked for forgiveness and read out the letter before presenting it to him. For a while, he just stood looking at it and I wondered what was going through his mind. When he spoke, he was choking back the tears. He said how moved and honoured he felt and that he had never experienced anything like this before. It was evident that God had really touched him.

The process of healing had begun and we know that God loves this land so much that He will continue His work long after we have left! As it says in Philippians (Chapter 1 v 3-6); *"I thank my God every time I remember you. In all my prayers for all of you, I always pray with joy because of your partnership in the gospel from the first day until now, being confident of this, that he who began a good work in you will carry it on to completion until the day of Christ Jesus."*

Chapter Seventeen
Remembering the King

During the months that had led up to our return trip to Drogheda and Wexford, I had felt the Holy Spirit's prompting to look again at the beheading of King Charles I. I had always known this was a wrongful act which had affected not only our area, but had also impacted our nation. It was certainly an act we should apologise for, which is why I had previously written to the Queen. However, it wasn't until now that I began to understand more fully.

One evening, as Annette, Vanessa and I were praying about the apathy towards prayer in our area. The scripture from Isaiah 1 v 15 was given to us, "*When you spread out your hands in prayer, I will hide my eyes from you. Even if you offer many prayers, I will not listen. Your hands are full of blood.*" This scripture was given to God's rebellious people and it was a hard word for us too, but somehow we knew that God was pointing us towards something.

As we continued to pray, I remembered that in Huntingdon on the site of Cromwell's birthplace stands a private hospital. Inside still hangs a copy of the King Charles I death warrant, signed by Cromwell and others, on display like a trophy. It always seemed wrong to me that this should be treated as if it was something the people of Huntingdon should be proud of. A few days earlier, a friend of Vanessa's had just visited Parliament, where she said the original warrant was on display. It all began to make sense. If the beheading of the King by his subjects was an act of rebellion, then our Parliament today has rebellion at its root. We decided that before we met again, we would test this by fasting, praying and seeking God.

One day the following week, Annette was given the scripture from Lamentations 3 v 40-44. It wasn't a passage she was familiar with, in fact she said it wasn't a book she would normally think of reading. It reads, "*Let us examine our ways and test them, and let us return to the Lord. Let us lift up our hearts and our hands to God in Heaven, and say; we have sinned and rebelled and you have not forgiven. You have covered yourself with anger and pursued us. You have covered yourself with a cloud so that no prayer can get through.*" She felt her faith rise up and knew that this was God-given.

That evening, as we read this scripture together, we were reminded once again of John Mulinde's prophecy from Isaiah 60 v 1-3. God had shown him a thick dark cloud that was covering the people of Britain and Europe. We were beginning to understand. This time in our history had not only affected Britain, but also Europe. King Charles I was married to a French Catholic Princess, Henrietta Maria. This in itself caused great conflict as many believed that the King would be influenced by his Catholic wife. Also there was no law in England that would allow the King to be put on trial. However, a Dutch lawyer, Dr Isaac Dorislaus, who was appointed Legal Adviser to his trial, found an old Roman law that would allow them to go ahead. Was this manipulation once again?

We felt sure God was showing us that this act of rebellion was one of the reasons that this cloud was there. As we looked again at Lamentations and the scripture from Isaiah 1 v 15, we realised that both passages spoke of judgement from God on the land of Israel and Judah for their rebellious way. What was God trying to say to us?

All this happened at the time that Tony Blair, our Prime Minister of the day, was deciding whether to go to war on Iraq. Members of Parliament (MPs) from his own party, as well as from all sides of Parliament were, as the media called it, "in rebellion". People from around the country were demonstrating against the idea. They believed that this was wrong and that once again, we would have blood on our hands. Will their voices be heard? Were Jeremiah's tears on behalf of his land heard? Or, like the people of Israel and Judah, will we once again reap what we have sown? We knew without a doubt, that just as we had been called to address the issue of Cromwell in Ireland, we were also being called to address King Charles I's execution. We prayed that if we had heard God right and He wanted us to deal with this, that He would open the door and give us the people He wants to use.

The next morning the telephone rang. I couldn't believe my ears, it was the Rev Mark Mills-Powell. About a year earlier, Mark had telephoned me and asked if I would go and pray with him, as he had just moved into the area. Although we had spoken on the phone, I had only met him the once when Annette and I had gone to pray with him in Linton. Mark had asked what we had been doing and I told him of our involvement in the Cromwell reconciliation work. As I was talking, Mark jumped up from his chair with great excitement and reached up to get a book from his shelf. He placed it on the table in front of me. "This," he said "is one of my ancestors." I looked at the cover. It was entitled *Only in Heaven. The life and Campaigns of Sir Arthur Heselrige 1601-1661*. Mark went on. "Sir Arthur was one of Cromwell's leading men." Annette and I had looked at each other with astonishment. This had all happened about twelve months earlier. I hadn't heard from Mark from that day until now, the day after our prayer for God to give us the right people if He wanted us to address the King's execution.

As soon as I heard Mark's voice, I remembered him telling us that Sir Arthur was one of the men who refused to sign the King's death warrant. Wow, I thought what are the chances of this happening unless God was in it?

A day or two later Vanessa telephoned me very excited. "Have you seen the programme coming on television this week? It's called "Blood on our Hands" - it's all about the execution of King Charles I." I was speechless, as I was reminded of the scripture in Isaiah 1 v 15 *"your hands are full of blood."* Once again God was using the media to show us that we were on track. I am very aware that there were many injustices and sins committed by both Royalists and Parliamentarians during the Civil War. King Charles I, like Cromwell, was guilty of gross misconduct. However, no matter how deep the conviction, executing the King was not the right way to resolve the differences.

Our next step was to do more research. I decided that a good place to start would be to read the accounts of the trial. I discovered that 135 judges were to try the King, but only 68 turned up. The rest did not wish to be involved. MPs who were against putting the King on trial were prevented from entering Westminster, on the orders of Oliver Cromwell. In fact, the only people allowed in were those Cromwell thought supported him. This was manipulation and control at its worst. However, of the 46 MPs allowed in, only 26 voted in favour of putting the King on trial.

Cromwell has always been known as the "Father of democracy". Was this democracy? Cromwell believed that he was doing the will of God. However, we serve a Just and Holy God, not one who manipulates things to get His own way. From this act of rebellion and control, our government was formed. That is its root. If this great sin goes unrepented of, it will go on affecting future leaders. God wants a righteous government, a government that is built on truth and justice. King Charles I, who was executed on January 30th 1649, never recognised the authority of the trial. He is quoted to have said "*I would know by what power I am called hither. I would know by what authority, I mean lawful, there are many unlawful authorities in the world. Remember, I am your King, your lawful King, **and what sins you bring upon your heads, and judgement of God upon this land.** Think well upon it, I say, think well upon it, before you go further from one sin to a greater. I have trust committed to me by God, by old and lawful descent, I will not betray it, to answer a new unlawful authority.*" Powerful words!

This happened eight months before Cromwell's invasion of Ireland. I wonder if he would have continued with the invasion had the King still been alive. As I had already written and apologised to our Queen in 2002, I had no idea what the next stage would be. We just had to wait for God's leading.

The Falcon Inn on Huntingdon market square was once the headquarters of Cromwell and his men. So, one summer's day we decided to go and have lunch there. As you would expect, the inn was full of memorabilia of the Civil War. One picture in particular caught my eye. It was of Cromwell, robed in royal garments, being handed the sword of state. The inscription underneath read, "*The inauguration of Oliver Cromwell as Lord Protector, when Oliver Cromwell, on June 26th 1657, caused himself to be invested as Lord Protector, King Edward's chair was for the first and only time in its history, removed from Westminster Abbey to Westminster Hall. He is here seen being girded with the sword of state.*"

In the end, Cromwell became everything he had fought against. He was crowned King in everything but name, and took the throne without godly authority. What also stood out to me in the picture was Cromwell being handed the sword of state. I was reminded that God had placed in my hand the sword of the spirit, His word. It is only God's sword that can restore the Crown and the Government, which had both been affected by this sinful act.

It was now 2004 and although it was months since God started to give us revelation about the King's execution, we had never stopped praying for His guidance. One day I received a teaching tape called "The Redemptive Gift of England" by Arthur Burk. Arthur shares that over the centuries, many have tried to rule England without the King, Church or State and failed. This was what Arthur called 'raw power'. He explains that in the time of the Puritans (Cromwell's time) they, like many others in history, used raw power to achieve their own ends. God intended the Church, the Government and the Monarchy to be in unity, each playing their part to bring about a moral authority. In the past, when all three have stood together, we saw the righteousness of God prevail in the land. The more I listened to this, the more it confirmed what we were doing. We were dealing with the results of what raw power had done centuries ago, that affected these three areas.

I recognise that at the beginning what Cromwell had in his heart was for a just, fair and godly land. However, this view was tainted by ideals he had inherited from his forebears. His Puritan prejudices and power took over. The King's trial and execution were the last straw and brought further division, even among his own men. Jesus talks in Luke 11 v 17, how *"A kingdom divided against itself will be ruined, and a house divided against itself will fall"*. Cromwell made sure that only those who agreed with him were allowed into the King's trial. This wasn't righteous or just, it was "raw" power. By owning and repenting of this, it could be a turning point in the history and healing of this nation. I felt we should go to London and pray at the site of the execution.

Summer was approaching when Mark asked us one day if we had heard that John Mulinde was one of the speakers at a local conference. Vanessa and I looked at each other and I knew she was thinking the same as I was. We both wanted to go. As a team, we had all gone through a very dry period and each of us was in need of some manna from God. He didn't disappoint us.

Meeting up with John again was one of my highlights. I remember well the first evening he addressed the conference, because God started to speak to me through him. He said how when he first came to England he found it so hard. In Uganda, they had always looked on England as their mother country, and yet it seemed to be so spiritually dry. He went on to say that in John 15, Jesus says *"Abide in me and I will abide in you"*. We all need to learn how to abide in Him and allow His presence to fill our homes. It is there that we need to give godly instruction. "Let your children see your passion. Let them see you cry to the Lord. This will teach them where to go when they are at breaking point. They will see you are not strong in yourself, but that you too need to draw strength from the presence of the Lord."

This reminded me how when my own children were young, we would come together to read the Bible and pray every night. Tears ran down my face as I remembered those times with fondness, and the joy I felt as I listened to our children talking to Jesus. I might not always have done it perfectly, but I had done my best to give them a good foundation to build upon. John invited us to rededicate our homes and families to God. This I did. I remember standing first and then kneeling, crying so much that I thought I would never stop as I felt His love pour over me. I hadn't realised how long I had been there until I turned around and nearly everyone had gone, except Annette and Vanessa.

"John's waiting to see you," Annette said as I sat down beside her. "He is over there talking, he didn't want to interfere with what God was obviously doing." A few moments later, John joined us. As we stood and chatted, catching up on the news, I felt again a stirring in me to return to Africa. I tried to ignore it when John said "As you know, next year Africamp is celebrating its tenth anniversary. Seeing you here tonight reminded me that you were one of the first to come. I would love it Shirley, if you would come back and share with us what God has been doing in your life since then." You could have knocked me down with a feather! "I would love to," I replied, "I have always known that one day I would return and I had always hoped that I would be able to share. So for you to ask me is incredible."

That night, Annette and I could hardly sleep, we were so excited. We were like two schoolgirls, giggling and laughing. The next morning, I knew I wouldn't be able to settle until I had spoken to Tony. Tony is very fond of John, and as I expected, he had no problem with me going, as long as I could find the money. Well, God had that in hand too. Before we had left the camp less than two days later, God had not only confirmed this call, but also given us the money for the flight!

Just to make sure we knew this call was from God, John spoke the next morning from Ezekiel 22 v 30; "*I looked for a man among them who would build up the wall, and stand in the gap on behalf of the land so that I would not have to destroy it, but found none.*" Thinking of Nehemiah rebuilding the walls of Jerusalem, John asked God

"What is this wall?" God showed him that the wall was there to protect His people against their enemies. All too often we ask God to bless us and pour out His spirit, even though we have not obeyed Him and kept His laws. The wall of God's blessing has been broken down by the many things that come between us and God, both as individuals and as a nation. "What we need to do is not focus on the problem but seek His face and His will. Pray and fast, wait for the breakthrough and for Him to show the way. Are you willing to stand in the gap and ask God the question, "What is in the way of us knowing your blessing in our land? What is the wall that needs to be rebuilt?"

When the invitation came for prayer, I left my seat straight away. A lady came to me and very gently said "God told me to say that you are a lovely rose, continue to bloom for Him." There's that rose again! I felt His love and I knew without doubt that God had spoken to me. I went home feeling refreshed and ready for the path ahead.

The time spent at the conference had reaffirmed our belief that the execution of King Charles I had caused a dark cloud over our land and further afield. Once the King was dead, Cromwell was able to concentrate on the invasion of Ireland. This brought death and destruction to so many, and thousands of Irish people were taken and sold to slave ships and sent to far distant lands. We have to thank God that despite all this, He still used this nation in the years that followed to take the Gospel into the world. Nevertheless, alongside the gospel, we also exported our divisions, especially those between Catholic and Protestant.

As the issue of King Charles I's death is addressed and repented of, I believe the part of the wall that was broken down centuries ago will be rebuilt and the cloud that comes between us and God will be removed. This will also allow the spiritual atmosphere over this nation to change. The spirit of death, rebellion and division will be replaced with a spirit of life and true unity. Unity, in which surrendering to one another allows us the freedom to seek the life that Christ longs to give us. Will this mean that we will have a perfect government? Of course not, because God will never take away our free will. However, if the bad root is dug out, then it cannot bear bad fruit anymore.

During the time we were praying about this, many things came into the light within government that are unjust and unholy. Even today as I write this, I have been listening to a programme on the radio in which a lawyer likened the trial and death of King Charles I to the manipulation he felt is still happening in modern government. He was talking about how the government was rushing through legislation to allow Parliament to hold terrorist suspects for months without charge. He went on to say that "Cromwell made sure the King's trial went his way and the same thing was happening all over again. We cannot allow laws to be made just to suit our own cause." I couldn't believe what I was hearing. Once again, God used the media to bring confirmation. God wants a righteous government.

Many Christians have spoken to me about their confusion over this issue and I understand this. However, if we believe God is holy and righteous, He would never ask anyone to do anything against His character. So, my question is, was manipulating the trial and execution of the King just, holy or righteous? The answer has to be no, this is not the character of God.

We knew we had to deal with this issue, but the question still was, "When?" As the King was executed on January 30th, this seemed to be the obvious date. As usual, I wanted to be sure, so I started to do more research. I have always believed that what we were doing was for Cromwell's family too. So you can imagine my astonishment when I found that it was on the same date, January 30th, in 1661, that Cromwell's body was exhumed from his grave in Westminster Abbey and posthumously hung, drawn and quartered. I believe that God wants to bring healing to all people from both sides. Cromwell's family, whether they have been aware of it or not, have also lived under this cloud for over 350 years and it's time that they too were set free. I was sure that we had picked the right date and as we would be returning from Uganda only a few days prior to the 30th, this seemed ideal.

With the date now fixed, the next step was to once again write to Her Majesty the Queen, the Prime Minister and other leaders telling them of our intentions. I believe that anything which affects so many people, as this does, should be done in the light, and not behind peoples' backs, especially leaders. So we wrote and within two weeks I was honoured to receive another reply from Buckingham Palace. The letter said the Queen was interested to learn of what we were doing and thanked us for bringing the date to her attention. She also thanked us for the assurance of our prayers.

Even though we were busy preparing to go to Uganda, we all realised how important it was to get together with Mark, hopefully in London, to pray about January 30th. Thankfully, God had His hand on it. Mark is a member of a club in Whitehall and he offered to reserve a room for us to use. This was perfect! God did say He was going to take us to places we normally wouldn't go, and this was certainly one of them! As we entered the hallway and walked up the grand marble staircase, I felt overwhelmed by God's generosity. Mark was waiting for us at the top. "Come with me," he said "I want to show you something." He led us into the members lounge where, in central place, was a statue of John Hampden. Hampden, with Sir Arthur Heselrige, was another of the men known as the "Five that flew." Back on January 3rd 1642, King Charles I demanded that these two men along with three others; John Pym, Denzil Holles and William Strode, be arrested for treason. It was the King's belief that these men had been encouraging the Scots to invade England and stirring up riots against him. So a messenger was sent to the House of Commons demanding their arrest. The House refused to comply with the King's demands because it was believed to be an infringement of their parliamentary privilege. So on 4th January, Charles took a body of men to the House of Commons himself, but he soon realised his five "birds had flown". The men had escaped. To this day it still influences the State Opening of Parliament in England. Black Rod is a senior officer in the House of Lords and is sent to the Commons Chamber to summon MPs to hear the Queen's Speech. Traditionally the door of the Commons is slammed in Black Rod's face to symbolise the Commons' independence from the Monarch. So you see how that part of history still affects us in the UK today.

We had an amazing time of worship that day. God's presence just came and filled the room. As we sat, not wanting to spoil the moment, we realised that just like the "five that flew", there were five of us around the table. Vanessa mentioned that only the day before she had been talking to someone about a sermon she'd heard on how David took five stones when he went out to kill Goliath. "In the sermon," she said "each stone was given a name, such as love or compassion, which are the weapons God gives us to fight with."

We were reading Psalm 45, which was the same Psalm that God used to direct us to write to the Queen back in 2002. As we read it again, we felt God was giving us the weapons with which to fight this battle. Verses 4 7 say, *"In your majesty ride forth victoriously on behalf of **truth**, **humility** and **righteousness**. Let your right hand display awesome deeds. Let your sharp arrows pierce the hearts of the king's enemies, let the nations fall beneath your feet. Your throne, oh God, will last forever and ever, a sceptre of **justice** will be the sceptre of your kingdom. You love righteousness and hate wickedness."* I had previously read the story of Sir Arthur and what was clear was that he was a man of integrity. So as his descendant, Mark would stand for **integrity**. Now we had the five:

Truth in place of deceit
Humility in place of pride and rebellion
Righteousness in place of wickedness
Justice in place of injustice
Integrity in place of manipulation.

We knew that like David, we would be doing battle for our land. So, we decided that on our return in January, each of us would bring a stone to represent these five foundations. Then after an act of repentance and Holy Communion, we would use them to build an altar to God at the site where the King died, to symbolically replace the old foundation of rebellion and death with a new one of humility and life. 1 Peter 2 v 4, 5 *"As you come to Him, the living Stone rejected by men but chosen by God and precious to Him you also, like living stones, are being built into a spiritual house to be a holy priesthood."*

During all this time, I felt God prompting me again to get started on this book. "You haven't given me a writer yet," I found myself crying out fearfully. "No, because nobody else can put your passion into it," came the reply. Oh dear I thought, I know that's true, but when I think about writing, it still terrifies me! Over the next day or two, I thought long and hard about this. I felt God reveal to me that I had cursed myself. Because all my life I had said, "I can't write, I am useless at spelling, don't ask me to write, I will only mess it up." I had believed this and it had almost become like a get-out clause, an excuse for not being obedient. Yes things had been said to me at school and at home that endorsed my low opinion of my abilities, but I still had a choice. I could either listen to what I and others had said, or I could listen to God and what He says to me, *"I can do everything through him who gives me strength."* (Philippians 4 v 13). I knew which it had to be. "OK God, if that's what you want then I am going to rely on you to help me. That day, I sat down at the computer and as you can read, our God was faithful. I know it is to His glory that you are reading this book now.

Chapter Eighteen
Africamp revisited

With Christmas behind us once again, we could start to concentrate on our Ugandan adventure. Although I was speaking at Africamp, I felt this wasn't the only reason we were going. The first time I went to Uganda was to witness the repentance and prayer, and the President handing the flag over as a sign of handing the nation back to God. Last time, it was to meet Bill Roy and the beginning of my Irish journey. What could it be this time, I wondered? Somehow our connection with Uganda had remained strong. What we didn't know was that God had yet another connection He wanted us to make.

That week as we gathered for prayer, Vanessa showed us an article from the newspaper on 1st January 2005. Under the Thirty Year Rule, each January official records from thirty years earlier are made public. The timing for this article to be released was extraordinary. We were stunned to read:

What Idi would have told the IRA

President Idi Amin of Uganda offered his services as peace broker in Northern Ireland. It may go down as the most unlikely attempt ever to broker a settlement to Northern Ireland's long-running troubles. In the middle of 1974, one of the worst years of the conflict, Uganda's dictator General Idi Amin stepped in with an offer to mediate between the two sides. The brutal and erratic Amin wrote to (Prime Minister) Harold Wilson suggesting he could host peace talks in his country. "It appears that the political and security situation in Northern Ireland is becoming worse every passing day without any feasible solution to it in sight." Amin wrote. "This serious and regrettable development calls for Britain's best and sincere friends to come to her assistance. Consequently, I avail my good offices at the disposal of the opposing sides in Northern Ireland. I suggest that representatives of your Catholic and Protestant communities in Northern Ireland as well as representatives of your government come to Uganda, far away from the site of battle and antagonism, for a conference on how to bring peace to their province." In a covering note, the British High Commission in Kampala said that, while the offer showed Amin's "naive view of world affairs", it was nevertheless "a genuine and sincere effort to be helpful."

Thinking back, it was Uganda that God used to point me in the right direction. It was the Ugandan President He used to speak to me about the healing of our land. It was Uganda He used to bring Bill Roy and I together. It seemed ironic that on the eve of going to Uganda again, I was reading how thirty years ago, Idi Amin tried to be part of the solution to Irish problems. I felt as though God was showing me His intention was always to use Uganda, but not that way. One day, everyone will see that God alone, through Jesus Christ, brings peace and reconciliation.

The day of our departure arrived. It was early morning when we came into land at Entebbe airport. I had always flown at night before so this time to be able to see Lake Victoria from the air was magnificent. After retrieving our baggage, we made our way to the exit. I hadn't managed to get in touch with Beth in Kampala before we left, so I wasn't sure if we were going to be able to stay with her. I had spoken to John about this and he had said it would be sorted out. So when someone approached us from Trumpet Mission (John's church) saying that a taxi had been arranged to take us to the hotel, we got in.

After a short journey, we pulled up outside a very nice, but very expensive hotel. It was here we met Milly. She was a real blessing and the best gift God could have given us at this time. She told us that Beth had been having a few problems so we were unable to stay with her until the following week. So she had reserved rooms for us in a cheaper hotel the other side of Kampala.

The following day, we attended the opening ceremony of the conference. This was extremely colourful with singing and dancing as we were entertained by a variety of children, many of whom were orphans. After introductions, one by one the government ministers rose to their feet and gave testimony to what God had done in their lives. It was thrilling to hear and lifted my spirit. The first time I came to Uganda God spoke to me saying "What you see me do here I can do where you are too." Well, I still believe this will happen and listening to all these testimonies filled me with even greater faith.

After all the dignitaries had gone, Pastor Rose came to inform me, that like all visiting speakers, I had been assigned a prayer partner while I was in Uganda. "I will introduce you to yours later," she said, "her name is Annette." I could hardly believe what I was hearing. I have always recognised that my friend Annette was not only a prayer partner but that she too plays a key role in this story. Now God was giving me double portion of prayer power with two Annettes!

Over the next few days, the teaching, testimony and ministry were excellent. Once again, John used the scripture *"If my people, who are called by my name, will humble themselves and pray and seek my face, and turn from their wicked ways, THEN will I hear from heaven, forgive their sin and heal their land."* John emphasised that it's the THEN that's important. When we have done all, THEN God says I will come and heal your land. "That is why so many prayers go unanswered," he said "because we haven't done the former part and humbled ourselves, prayed and sought His face with all that we have, and turned from our wicked ways. We seem to just expect to pray and God will do whatever we ask, despite our sin or regardless of our motive."

A few days later, we met up with Beth and her nephew Michael. I was so pleased to see her again, although she looked thin and fragile. I felt quite concerned that having us to stay would put more pressure on her and her family. However, this didn't seem to make any difference, as she kept apologising for the delay. She said that she had been going through a rough time and needed to get away for a while and be alone with God. "Also," she continued "I am afraid we have no water at the house. We have been unable to pay the bill for some time, so the water was cut off. We have to fetch it from down the road." Oh dear, I thought, we can't put this family through the worry of having us there as well. "However," she continued "when I told the family that you wanted to come and stay, they all said yes they must come, and we will do the work. So everyone has worked really hard to prepare your rooms. If you don't mind things not being quite the same, we would love you all to come and stay tomorrow."

This was a large household with Beth, her sisters and brothers, nephews and nieces and others, including a six-week-old baby. For the three of us to be there too would put a terrific burden onto them. Yet they were prepared to do this, and open their doors and their hearts to us once again. How would we ever be able to thank them?

As Beth had to work every day, this meant a different member of the family would join us for breakfast. One morning, Christine joined us. She had worked for the family for some time but couldn't speak English, so one of the family interpreted for her. We all sat amazed as we listened to her heart-wrenching story. "I was dying of AIDS and so ill, with sores all over my body," she said showing us the scars. "My eight-year-old daughter was told that I would die, so she went out and dug my grave." This was hard to listen to, we couldn't imagine what this lady and her child had gone through. She continued, "The family here were so good and believed that God would heal me. So they fasted and prayed for many weeks. God was faithful." Then lifting her hands up to Heaven she added

"Praise God, I am healed." At the conference, we heard more stories like Christine's. Many people testified how they had been healed from HIV and AIDS. Each one, including Christine, had medical proof of this.

The following morning, I was told I would be speaking that afternoon. Ever since I started on this journey, I have been aware that we are in a battle. Ephesians 6 v 12 tells us, "*For our struggle is not against flesh and blood, but against the rulers, against authorities, against the power of this dark world and against spiritual forces of evil in the heavenly realms.*" Many times over the years, I have felt the full force of this, as the enemy tried to distract and disturb me. This day was to be no different.

I had spoken to large numbers before, but never this many. There must have been around 4,000 people in the marquee that day. I began by explaining the principles of Wholeness Through Christ (WTC) before going on to tell my story. However, it wasn't long before things started to go wrong and the microphone went dead. I didn't know if I should carry on or not. Thankfully, one of the Pastors invited me to sit down and a time of worship filled the gap while it was fixed. It didn't take long and I was invited back onto the stage. However, once again, as soon as I got to the part in the story about John coming to England, the sound went dead again. This happened several times. It became obvious to everyone that this was a spiritual battle. The enemy didn't want me to speak.

The Pastor once again stepped up on the stage and encouraged everyone to pray and worship the Lord. "We are in a battle here this afternoon," he said "so get to your feet and let's pray and break its power in the name of Jesus." Everyone immediately stood up and started to declare to the heavenly realm that the victory belongs to Jesus Christ.

A group of ladies joined me and as we walked up and down the stage praying, I felt the Holy Spirit prompting me. This anointing became very heavy and I knew that sound or no sound, I just had to speak out. So at the top of my voice, I shouted and declared that I felt that the sound system going dead was a sign from God that England is being kept silent. The devil doesn't want England to have a voice like it used to have in the days of the missionaries. Our enemy has kept us silent for too long, we need your help. We need your faith because ours is weak. We need your prayers, ours have dried up. We need you to partner with us and pray for the release of England's voice again. England is asleep. Will you pray for her to wake up and come into her true inheritance? Please will you stand with us, will you stand and pray for us?"

It took over two hours for everything to get back to normal so I could continue. This was the only time during the conference that the sound system failed. I continued to tell the story, but with all the interruptions, I wasn't sure how long I had been speaking. I knew I had to bring it to a close, so I finished by telling everyone that I was writing a book, and that if they wanted to know the full story, they would have to wait till it was published.

People were free to come and talk afterwards. Gottfried Bernard, one of the German interpreters, came rushing towards me. "Shirley," he said, "you have no idea what God has done here today, you have really touched my heart. You said you are writing a book. Can I ask who is going to publish it for you?" I told him that I hadn't even given this a thought. "Please would you allow me the privilege of translating your book into German?" I was quite taken aback, I hadn't expected anything like this. God just kept surprising me! I was aware that others were waiting to speak to me, so I asked if he would mind talking about this with Vanessa, who I knew spoke German. It wasn't until much later that I found out that he himself is a publisher.

A young man named Joseph came to speak to me. This humble man, like so many others, really touched us, as each came to tell us that they felt God's call to become an intercessor and cry out for England. Before the end of the conference, Joseph came and knelt in front of me. "Pastor," he said, placing a silver coin in my hand, "this is my covenant with you. I promise that from this day on, I will continue to pray for you and England." Tears welled up in my eyes. People in Uganda have so little. I knew that giving me this coin was a costly thing to do. However, I also knew the love and commitment with which it had been given. It wasn't until later that I remembered the article in the newspaper just before we left England. Had God always intended to use Uganda to help bring a breakthrough in the United Kingdom?

The following morning, Gottfried met me outside the marquee. "Shirley I have a gift for you. You touched my heart so much yesterday that I was up in the night asking God how I can show you what you have done. I felt Him tell me to give you this," he said as he passed me a large bag of red jelly hearts. I felt a little embarrassed as I took them from him, not knowing quite what to say. Vanessa had told me that he was quite a joker, so I replied, "It looks by this, as if lots of hearts were touched." With a twinkle in his eye he said, "That's exactly what God told me to tell you!"

At one point, Vanessa and I went outside to get a breath of fresh air and were joined by a young lady, Jovelet. As we sat on the grass, she told us her story. "When you spoke yesterday, I felt this sadness inside. I was abandoned when I was only eight, and this still makes me very sad. I have been crying all night asking God to help me." Her story was like thousands of others and I knew that we couldn't help them all. However, I remembered the story of the boy who while picking starfish up from the beach and throwing them back into the water, was approached by a man who told him, "There are thousands of starfish on this beach son, what you are doing won't make any difference." The boy replied as he threw another one back into the sea, "Sir it will make a difference to that one!" I believed God wanted to make a difference to this child of His. I very gently put my arms around her, praying that the Lord would reveal His love to her in a new way. Not surprising God answered that prayer and it has been a real joy to keep in touch with her and see what God has done over the years.

Sunday morning, we decided to take things easy and sat around chatting before going to Prayer Mountain later. We all love Beth and her gentle and quiet spirit and we were concerned for her when she admitted she was feeling spiritually dry. All the time we had been staying at the house, we had wanted to pray with Beth about the water situation, but we didn't want to embarrass her. However, today it seemed was the right time. So we asked if she would like us to pray with her. As we did, I felt that the lack of water in the home was like a prophetic sign of the dryness she was feeling. The enemy had robbed her and this family of the fullness of God's love for so long that this made me angry. The enemy had robbed her and this family for too long and it made me angry. So we declared in the name of Jesus that he would restore everything to them. We prayed for the living water of Jesus to flow again in her life. I asked the Lord to give Beth a sign so that she would know this was from Him. Two days later after our evening meal, Beth said she had a surprise for us. She had received a letter from the Kampala water board, granting her an amnesty and the water would be reconnected free of charge! The living water was flowing again! Not only was Beth set free, but the whole family was blessed as well.

The next few days on Prayer Mountain were to be for me both inspirational and personal as God encouraged me over and over again. Prayer Mountain is a very special place where you can feel God's presence in a unique way. While I sat looking over the city, the thought came that I should take one of the stones from the mountain to London for our prayer altar.

Later that day, John Mulinde asked to see me. John and I have known each other for a long time and he is a great encouragement to me. While we talked together, I told him about how God had led us to London and about building an altar with His righteous stones. "I feel God has prompted me to ask if we could take one from here. I believe that this place represents the prayer foundation that the Christians of Uganda have built upon and I believe God wants us to do the same."

It was with great sadness that we said goodbye to our friends as we left Prayer Mountain. One by one they said farewell, pledging to pray for us. One lady told me that every night between 12 midnight and 3 in the morning she would be praying for England. Another promised to pray without ceasing. Another told me that she would pray for Ireland. My goodness, there is so much we could learn from these dedicated people!

Chapter Nineteen

Laying New Foundations

Even though I was sure that God had spoken to us about the blood guilt and rebellion brought on the land by executing the King, the week after our return from Uganda was yet another time of testing. The 30th of January 2005 was a Sunday and we were off to Westminster. Mark joined us directly after morning worship, so I wasn't surprised that he was still wearing his black clergy cloak and Canterbury hat. However, when he kept it on, I did think it was a bit strange. I was to find out later that this was a deliberate act on his part. He told me, "I am wearing this today, dear Shirley, not to make me look good, but because I think it's important that people can see the authority we have."

Although I knew what we were doing was part of God's plan, at the same time the doubts still kept coming. Who do you think you are? What difference will it make going to London? Why couldn't you have prayed at home? I felt as if I was in a battle for my mind. I shared my feelings in the car and I was relieved to know I wasn't alone. Mark, the great encourager, heard us talking and immediately started to pray. After that, we prayed on and off for the rest of the journey. Things had been difficult for me and I remember distinctly praying, "If this is Your will today Lord, please confirm it with a sign before we go home."

It wasn't until we were outside Westminster Palace that we realised none of us knew exactly where the Banqueting Hall was. In my naivety, I had thought it would be obvious, but it wasn't. Once Mark had asked for directions, we discovered that we had a short walk down Whitehall. Mark and I were quite a distance ahead of the others when we were approached by two people handing out leaflets. Nothing unusual in that you might think. However, when I looked at mine and Mark at his, we couldn't believe what we saw. One sheet had a picture of Cromwell, with "Republic" written at the top with a tick beside it. On the other was a list of reasons for abolishing the Monarchy. Isn't God amazing? I had asked Him to confirm what we were doing and He had! We knew without doubt this rebellious spirit was still active in the land.

With security in London being tight, we didn't know if we would be allowed to stand for any length of time outside the Banqueting Hall, let alone hold a service there. However, once again it seemed that God had it in hand. The police passed by several times, glancing as they did so, but seemingly took no notice. Perhaps they recognised the authority in which Mark was dressed.

We all stood in a circle, as a symbol of our unity and a reminder of God's eternal love. After sharing scripture, Mark reminded us that it is because of the death and resurrection of Jesus that we are healed and reconciled to God. It was His blood, shed for all mankind that brought us back into a relationship with our Heavenly Father. And it is only by the same blood that history can be healed too. 1 Peter 1 v 18-19, "*For you know that it was not with perishable things such as silver and gold, that you were redeemed from the empty way of life handed down to you by your forefathers, but with the precious blood of Christ, a lamb without blemish or defect.*" We held these thoughts in our minds as we shared the bread and wine together.

We stood silent for a while before we prayed asking God's forgiveness for the death and destruction of the Civil War and in particular, the execution of the King. One by one, we laid down our stones as we built an altar of prayer, replacing the old foundations of death and rebellion with God's new ones of righteousness, truth, humility, justice and integrity.

This was all new to our driver and I wondered how he was coping, but he was fine. In fact, as we were finishing, he brought our attention to a group of people coming towards us, dressed in costumes from the Cromwell period. I wondered if they would ask what we were doing, but they didn't, they just passed by, looking before turning around and going back in the same direction. Then suddenly they were gone. Were they angels?

With our trip to London over, I wondered if this was now to be the end of our Cromwell journey. But, as we were to soon find out, it was to be yet another beginning.

However, that's another story.

Postscript, 2013

This story was to take an amazing turn in May 2011 when Her Majesty Queen Elizabeth II visited the Republic of Ireland for the first time. In her speech at Dublin Castle she said "With the benefit of historical hindsight we can all see things which we would wish had been done differently or not at all" Words that brought us to tears and deeply touched the nation. This is without doubt a clear sign of God's power to bring healing and restoration, and to God be all the glory!

I felt I had to write to her Majesty after this visit. Here is part of that letter; "Cromwell became Lord Protector of this nation by beheading King Charles I, which then enabled him to carry out his campaign in Ireland. Your Majesty, your visit as Sovereign of our nation sowed a godly seed back into that land as you went in the opposite spirit to that of Cromwell. Your humble and gentle spirit conveyed the healing that God is bringing to Ireland."

I received a reply from her Majesty from Balmoral Castle. The letter said how touched she was by the sentiments I had expressed and that it had been a real source of pleasure and encouragement to both her and the Duke of Edinburgh. They were most grateful for my thoughtfulness in writing as I did.

To God be all the glory!

Epilogue

In my travels, I have come to recognise that many people, and this may even be you, find this issue of Cromwell difficult to understand. He is, and I expect will always be, a controversial figure. Some see him as a godly man leading the country to freedom. Others see him as a dictator who had no thought or care for those who disagreed with him. It's not my job, nor the purpose of this book, to judge him or anyone else. God is the one and only judge of us all. However, when God points His finger at injustice, bloodshed and broken covenants, then it's our responsibility to be obedient to His calling. There are some things that time does not heal and if we lack the diligence and discernment to see what they are, then we can prevent ourselves and others from knowing God's blessing. God longs to pour out His Spirit on everyone. However, as I have tried to explain in this book, we have to face whatever offends God. Whether it was last year, ten years ago, 100 or 1,000, it makes no difference to Him. It still has to be dealt with.

As we draw to the end of this book, allow me to ask you a few questions. What has God been saying to you? Has He been revealing obstacles in your life or the life of your family? Or has He been showing you the need for healing in the church? Or has He revealed more of His heart for your nation? Only you know. However, my prayer for you is that by His love and grace you will hear Him saying to you "This is the way my dear child, walk with me and find healing."

Do you find this story incredible, almost too hard to believe? So do I. However, don't forget we are dealing with a God who never changes. The same God who created the heavens and the earth, who spoke with Moses from a burning bush, who caused the water to part so that His people could cross on dry land, who commanded Noah to build a boat far from the sea, who empowered Samson to have the strength of a whole army, who spoke again and again through His prophets to warn His people of their rebellion, who caused His own son Jesus to come to earth and share our human existence, who then empowered Him to heal the sick and raise the dead, whose love is so unconditional that He suffered and died for us. He is the same God who raised Jesus to life again. The same God who has made a way for us to spend eternity with Him and who sent His Holy Spirit to empower His disciples to go and do likewise. That's you and me!

Incredible! Unbelievable! Yes I agree, but then He is the God of the Bible!

Testimonies

W. Frank Godfrey, Mayor of Drogheda 2000
Malachy P. Godfrey, Mayor of Drogheda 2002

We wish to sincerely thank the team and the great gifts they bore of peace and reconciliation to the people of Drogheda. Their magnanimous apology for past wrongs by Oliver Cromwell and his army against the Drogheda populace in 1649 has been a healing balm and affords all of us the opportunity to move on in our lives in a more positive spirit. On the wider scale, the ever increasing levels of co-operation and neighbourliness between our two countries is further enhanced, and is fast blossoming into an abiding friendship and mutual respect, because of people like Arise Ministries reaching out the hand of peace and friendship.

We in Drogheda will forever cherish and deeply value the Arise visits to our historic town of Drogheda.

Le Mor Meas.
(You are held in great respect.)

Augustine Reay (Gussy),
Holy Family Prayer Group, Drogheda

I first met Shirley and her friends when they visited Drogheda in March 2002. They came to us from The Christian Renewal Centre at Rostrevor, a place our prayer group hold in high regard. Shirley told us how the inspiration for retracing Cromwell steps came through prayer. We felt sure this was from God, so we organized a reception and prayer walk in our town, which members of the Borough Council and the Mayor attended. As I write this letter, it was announced by the IRA that on the 26th September 2005, they had handed in their entire armoury and now wish to proceed with a political path. I don't say coming to Drogheda brought this about, but I do believe that it did no harm. In conclusion, I see that Shirley and her friends stepped out in faith and in doing so won the respect of our prayer group and those they met in Drogheda.

The Lord bless you, the Lord be kind and gracious to you. The Lord make His face shine on you and may the Lord give you peace.

In the name of Jesus.

Dr Janet Craven, Dublin

How vivid is my childhood memory of walking along beside a local ploughman, when he started talking about Cromwell. There was such vehemence in his voice, even in how he spoke the name it sounded like "Crumell". I can still sense the pain. As we learned our history, we heard the much remembered and fearful phrase "To Hell or Connaught". In recent years, I saw the maps of the Down Survey, 1654-56, of Ireland (minus Connaught, which I looked for in vain). I could find only three or four bridges across the Shannon's length. So what was it like for all those poor people?

A few years ago on a history walk with a group of cub scouts north of Dublin city, a field was pointed out where "Cromwell and his troops did such and such." So the folk memory is real and lives on. The enigma of the man with the Bible and his reportedly devout soldiers often puzzled me was there any answer?

Then I met David, doing my sister's garden, near Huntingdon. He said "You ought to meet Shirley Bowers" and I did sometime later. I was privileged to join the Arise Ministries team in Dublin and to walk, praying together, down O'Connell Street past his impressive statue, crossing O'Connell Bridge, on past Trinity College and Dublin Castle to the national Cathedral of St Patrick.

The responses from the team's visit to Ireland leave me in awe of the Lord God who makes all things well.

Marie Gough, Prayer leader, Dublin

To come to Ireland and offer repentance for what Cromwell had done in this land was no easy task. I believe this visit broke down strongholds of the enemy over the nation. When God's people do what He asks of them, the enemy's right to rule is taken from him.

The name Oliver Cromwell put a shudder in every Irish person's body. As we have learned the terrible stories in history, to be able to stand with our brothers and sisters from England and hear their hearts of love was indeed very healing. God exposes hidden areas of unforgiveness when confronted like this. I can now say I can hear Cromwell's name and it no longer affects me. It's ended, forgiven, let go.

Pat Murphy, Pastor, Wexford

Wexford Christian Fellowship feels that the Cromwell Steps Reconciliation Journey was strategic and also very beneficial in clearing the way for God to move. In general, we also found it a very moving experience. Furthermore we noticed a great openness to the Gospel in the period subsequent to the visits of the Arise team.

Stephen and Georgina Forbes, Wexford

We truly found it deeply touching that in 2002, English people would come to Ireland and apologise for a wound of history. It is truly godly and brings a tremendous and tangible blessing to all sides. Before God, unrepented sin remains just that, no matter when the action happened, until it is addressed by God's grace in repentance by the Spirit of God. The way the team asked for permission to enter our town the exact opposite of the manner in which Oliver Cromwell and his troops had entered Wexford in 1649, also deeply impacted us.

A very moving event took place in the Franciscan Friary in Wexford. The reconciliation prayer service was followed by a tangible effervescence in all those present, affecting even those who had only been invited to the service just a short few hours beforehand. We must also highlight the genuine emotion expressed by Shirley Bowers in the Parish Church of Courtnacuddy, in Co.Wexford. This is a parish where so many families have a story to tell about the Cromwell times. As Shirley spoke words of repentance to Fr Jim Finn in front of a large congregation, she shed tears and doubled over with grief, expressing heartfelt sorrow and remorse for the wounds of history which had been inflicted in the Courtnacuddy area.

In 2003, during the team's second visit to Co. Wexford, there were many moving moments. The one that we particularly remember was the visit of the team to the parish of Tomhaggard. There, the priest, Fr McDonald produced the actual chalice used by Fr Nicholas Mayler in the celebration of Christmas morning Mass, in 1653. This Mass proved to be the last for Fr Mayler, as Cromwell's troops descended on the gathering, killing him.

The visits of the team in 2002 and 2003 to Co. Wexford were a blessed experience of deep and worthwhile Christian fellowship which we will remember forever. It was a huge privilege to be involved with people from the Huntingdon area who are of such sterling and godly character, who came over to our country in an attitude of gentleness and readiness to be a blessing to us from the heart of God. They were also prepared to do "the difficult thing" and apologise. As descendants of "the abused party" even though it is so many years later, we are aware that the oppressions of history remain in one's psyche/spirit. These oppressions exert a negative and crushing influence which deeply affects the way we as a people, and even as individuals, think about ourselves and behave in our own lives.

We have always known that our God can and does heal wounds in our personal histories and we never doubted that He could and would heal the wounds of a nation's history. This was the right approach, inspired by the Father God Himself and empowered by the atoning death of Jesus and His resurrection. The scripture that comes to mind from the book of Acts sums this thought up; "*Repent ye, therefore that times of refreshing might come from the Lord.*" Acts 3 v 19.

We should also mention that responses on behalf of Irish people to English people, such as murderous thoughts, words and actions, were "underlined" by the Holy Spirit as matters needing repentance on our side. At no time is sin acceptable to a righteous, living God. The addressing of the sin by ourselves in an important way "completed the picture" and was a significant step of maturity for us in our Christian walk.

We thank our Father God for His faithful servants of Christ from around Huntingdon who were so sensitive to the thoughts and intents of the Lord's heart.

Joseph Kennedy, Secretary of Callan Heritage Society

Unfortunately I was away the day Arise Ministries came, but I can tell you the visit went over wonderfully well. I have not heard a single person say anything negative about the visit of reconciliation. It was most appreciated and on behalf of Callan Heritage Society, I thank you all most sincerely for your courage, honesty and goodness.

Peig O Loughlin, Kilkenny

May I thank you for coming to Kilkenny and taking up this vision. We are so thankful that God in His mercy is sending groups to heal the land from the past.

Fr Paddy Kenny, Kilconnell
(interviewed by Joy Daniels and Peig O Loughlin)

"The Arise team remembered Cromwell's sins, even the sins done in the name of God. They made a gesture of confession and repentance. They got personally involved. They prayed for forgiveness, even though it was not their sin. We are in an age of forgiveness. We are in an age of change. God forgives immediately and cleanses as we come and acknowledge the sin." Father Paddy also said he was thrilled to see such vibrant deep Christian faith and the fact that the group was interdenominational was an added bonus.

Tim Jenkinson, Cork

The Arise visit was very significant. We had been praying for a number of years for Cork, meeting each week. Sister Bridget mentioned she had been asked to host a group who were prayer walking around Ireland. We had no information on the group other than that. That same afternoon, we decided to plan a prayer walk around the route of the old city walls of Cork. I went to the library to get a map of the old city walls and as I looked through various books, two pieces of information struck me as being significant and both were related to a building our attention had previously been drawn to. We later learned this building was Queens Castle, one of two castles that made up the old main gate of Cork. The castle and gate are on the coat of arms of Cork. The two significant pieces of information were that Oliver Cromwell entered the city when the officer in command of Queens Castle opened the gates. Some years later, the castle was used as a jail with a courthouse above. The Catholic Bishop of Cork was being tried for his religion when the courtroom collapsed, killing some and leaving a chasm between the judge and the Bishop in the dock. As I reported back this information, I was amazed to learn that the prayer walkers were coming from Huntingdon, the home of Oliver Cromwell.

Some weeks later, I came across a book that well illustrated the legacy of Oliver Cromwell in Ireland. Before his arrival, Ireland had been the most religiously tolerant kingdom of the four kingdoms that made up the British Isles. He left it religiously polarised. He also personifies the nadir, or lowest point, of Irish history. Though not responsible for all Ireland's ills, he stands at that point in history where war, plague and famine had left the land desolate.

The great encouraging significance of your visit for me was that it spoke powerfully into my spirit that God had drawn a line in the sand, and was saying to us in this land, "The time of your hard service is over, winter is past and a new season is beginning."

God bless you for your faithfulness.

Tony Broderick, Athlone

In retracing the steps of Cromwell to various towns and cities, in the spirit of peace and reconciliation, we believe the team contributed greatly towards bringing an understanding of the necessity to voice forgiveness and regret for all the wrongs done to one another throughout history. In so doing, demonstrating the love of God, which was so evident in their communication with the local Catholic Community. We thank God for the spirit of grace and peace.

Phyllis Forsythe, Omagh, Northern Ireland

Ethel Moore and I are from Catholic and Protestant backgrounds. We have been praying together since the 1980's about the historical hurts of Ireland. It was an answer to our prayers that the Arise team came to Ireland to apologise for what Oliver Cromwell had done to the people of Ireland. It was a great honour for me to take part in the group's visits in 2002 and 2003. I really believe the situation in Ireland has changed for the better. I love this land and I pray that the people of Huntingdon and indeed all of England will be blessed mightily because of these acts of kindness.

Rev Edward Wright, Rochester, Kent

Those few days I spent with Arise Ministries on the Irish reconciliation trip in September 2002 gave me some of the most vivid emotional memories of my life. As we moved from one situation to another, it seemed that God had gone before us preparing hearts for the encounters we had, not least my own.

By way of background explanation, although I have lived in England all my life, my father's family were Anglo-Irish. One James Wright, reputedly the younger son of a family split by the Civil

War, had gone over as a Captain in Cromwell's army. I am sorry to say that he had taken land at the cost of blood. Not all the bloodshed was confined to distant history though. My father's sister was killed in Dublin during The Troubles in 1921 as she watched a cricket match. Some said it was a stray bullet, others that it was intended for someone next to her. There was a sense that the full truth never came out. I went on the trip with a personal awareness of the need for reconciliation and healing.

Shortly after arriving at the Renewal Centre at Rostrevor, we were enjoying warm Christian fellowship over a cup of tea with some of the people there. We were talking about the reason for our visit. During the conversation, I mentioned that my ancestor had come over in Cromwell's army. Those who say that 300-year-old history does not affect us should have seen the change brought about by the information I shared. Fellowship was lost. I hasten to add that it was soon restored when the lady came up to me the next day and asked for forgiveness for her attitudes and words, and of course these were freely given. However, it had been an early example of the force of feelings that are still strong, and of the need for the sort of trip that Arise Ministries had arranged. Later that day, after a time of talking and praying together as a group, I remember falling on my knees alongside an Irish Catholic lady, weeping and weeping and embracing. Pain and sorrow, even anguish, followed by warm, restorative healing, flowing very deep.

The vivid pattern of emotions surfaced again a day or two later at the civic reception in Drogheda. Shirley had undertaken the main business of reading the letters and she and others had made moving apologies. I felt a growing impulsion to go forward, and once more took to my knees, this time in front of the Mayor. I felt weighed down with shame and guilt. This wasn't a scheduled piece as such, or something I had planned or even thought through carefully. However, there was a very positive, open approach in Shirley's leadership, and it simply seemed the only proper way to give expression to what welled up inside me, and I would believe it was a response to the promptings of the Holy Spirit. The Mayor represented the city visited with such violence by Cromwell's men, and I felt I had to ask forgiveness from him. To his credit, he coped well with a gesture that could easily have seemed overdone. It might have all felt very awkward, but it wasn't on the contrary, the whole occasion seemed wonderfully releasing.

In St Peter's Church, where many were burned as the tower where they had taken refuge was set alight by Cromwell's men, there had been a fire more recently and the smell of burning still hung in the air. It gave a sense of the atrocity and outrage that had been perpetrated there, disturbing and moving, and we began to pray for God's mercy. I was carrying a small shofar (ram's horn) and asked the local minister if I could blow it as part of our appeal to God. The wailing sound a shofar can make expressed more effectively than words the burden I felt in that haunted atmosphere, and for me brought a touch of release.

The next day, we went to pray in the street at St Lawrence's Gate and moved, in an unplanned way, from praying to sharing bread and wine and then to washing one another's feet prayers in action, and signs of our desire to come in a spirit of healing and service, as opposed to bloodshed and domination. I saw it as reminding God of His promises, in faith that the blood of Christ speaks a better word than the blood unrighteously spilt on the land. I would usually feel some embarrassment at a spontaneous bout of foot-washing in the street, but I don't remember any. There seemed to be such a flow of the Holy Spirit that any reservations were over-ridden.

As Drogheda is known as a gateway to the nation, sitting as it does at the head of the River Boyne, there was a sense that while what we were doing was bringing cleansing and peace to the site of the atrocity, it could also have a significance beyond Drogheda. Perhaps it could be part of opening a gateway for healing to flow from there to other areas of the nation.

While staying near Drogheda, I met up with a distant cousin who lives in an adjacent street to St Lawrence's Gate. It turned out that two members of his immediate family are called Edward, like me, and one called Thomas, as is our eldest son which confirmed the link, remote though it was. When we first met, he greeted me saying, "Welcome home!" I was surprised how deeply this touched me. That could be said of the whole visit as far as I was concerned. It was altogether a truly healing experience for me personally, and more importantly, I believe significant seeds of reconciliation were sown. We continue to pray that the peaceable harvest of righteousness might increase in that land.

Rev Stephen Talbot,
formerly at Ashburnham Prayer Centre, East Sussex

I was only on the first part of the journey which involved the visit to Drogheda, but it represented a landmark in my walk with the Lord and was the culmination of years spent in praying for our own area around Huntingdon. Since John Mulinde came to St James Church, Hemingford Grey, in the mid 1990's with his message of how intercessory prayer could change nations, towns and areas, Shirley and myself with a group of like-minded Christians sought to implement his teaching and insight from the Bible. Step by step, God guided us as we learned more about history and how the spiritual was impacted by the historical. We shared our insight with a number of groups along the way some accepted the challenge and the new insights; others found it difficult to follow. God took us to Uganda to learn more and in 1999 we celebrated Cromwell's birthday in Huntingdon, but we also recognised his profound legacy of bloodshed and division through the Civil War.

God opened our eyes to all that had happened in Ireland and we knew there was important work to do in terms of reconciliation. So going to Drogheda was the culmination of years of work and prayer, travel and travail. I knew before I went to Drogheda that it was a gateway place, more in my spirit than through reading or research, so it was encouraging to find that the town's logo is actually a gateway. We visited St Lawrence's Gate and prayed there. It was wonderful to meet the people of Drogheda who recognised the legacy of the past and who earnestly wanted reconciliation too. It was a humbling moment when we met and prayed together. How faithful Jesus is when we follow Him, even when we don't understand the full significance of what we are doing! Now, we understand so much more and we know there is more to come.

I could not stay for the whole of the trip because of my work at Ashburnham, but I have come to a place which has the strongest possible links with King Charles I! This is yet another part of the ongoing journey whereby God wants to change the course of history today by dealing with the sins of the past. The Cromwell Reconciliation Journey was not just a landmark it was a turning point for all of us involved in walking with Jesus in seeking to bring healing to our land and the land of Ireland.

Annette Quail, Arise team member

I remember watching a news report in the early 1990's about the political situation in Ireland and saying to my husband that someone should try and put things right or the pain and frustration would just carry on from one generation to the next. I had married a man from Northern Ireland in 1981 and been over to Belfast a few times to visit his family. During that time, I heard all about "the troubles" and how this had affected them. I had a real desire to see things change, but what could I do?

For most of the 1980's and all of the 1990's, I had been attending Godmanchester Baptist Church in Cambridgeshire. One evening in 1997, two speakers from Hemingford Grey Church came to talk to us about setting up prayer altars in every town or village. Their names were Rev Stephen Talbot and Shirley Bowers. They had just returned from a prayer conference in Uganda. I could feel the excitement in my spirit as they were speaking, so at the end of the evening when Shirley invited anyone who would be interested in setting up a prayer cell in their village, I knew I had to be involved.

Over the next few months, I started to meet with Shirley and others to pray for Huntingdon and God began to talk to us about Cromwell and all that had taken place in Ireland. By the end of that year, not only was there a prayer cell in Brampton, but I was booked on the next Africamp in Uganda along with Shirley and Stephen. Africamp '98 was very different to the previous year. Even though we were enjoying the conference, we were not really sure why we were there. Then just a few days before we were due to return home, Shirley met a minister from a church in Northern Ireland and as they talked, it became clear that God had been talking to him about Oliver Cromwell and Ireland too. How amazing is that?

After many trips to Ireland, God had prepared us to undertake the Cromwell Reconciliation Journey. I have to say that it was a huge privilege to be carrying a letter of apology from the churches in Huntingdon to the towns in the Republic of Ireland that had been so affected by the actions of Cromwell and his army. As the letter was handed to the Christian and Civic leaders of each town, we were able to witness and take part in, genuine reconciliation between two nations and people groups. This is something I shall never forget and will always praise God for, as only He could do this.

Vanessa Murphy, Arise team member

It is an enormous privilege to be a part of this ministry. I have heard and read this story many times now, and each time I marvel at God's amazing plan unfolding in ways we couldn't begin to imagine. Indeed, we often say 'You couldn't make it up'!

My journey in this began when in May 2000, my family moved to St Ives in Cambridgeshire, a move that I knew at the time was God's plan. I met Shirley at a prayer meeting soon after, when she and Stephen Talbot commented on the number of people moving into the area with an Irish surname. I soon discovered it was no coincidence that I had married into a family with Irish Catholic roots and lived here. I felt as though I had stepped into my destiny. God has given me a longing to see healing in Ireland, in my own town and in my husband's family, and it is such a blessing to be a part of that process. I have witnessed God's touch on many people from all walks of life, from priests to mayors and housewives. Shirley and I have written letters to all manner of people, even the Queen. I marvel that this is my experience. I praise God for all that He has done and I bless Shirley for her unswerving obedience to the Lord.

Lance and Beryl Ayres, Arise Team members

Our visit to Ireland with Arise Ministries was a "Happening". We hadn't planned to go in the first instance. However, we were invited over to Ireland because of a baby left on our doorstep on the night of St Patrick's Day. From then on, we knew it was right. The Lord our God just showed us His agenda. We believe He is still completing the work which this visit began. We wouldn't have missed it for all the tea in China, anymore than letting a wheelchair dampen our spirits either!

Katie Sims, Arise Team member

When I first heard Shirley speak at a meeting on this subject, my heart leapt and I wanted to know more. So I arranged to meet with her to get the full story. This helped me understand who I was and how we as individuals and as a nation affect history.

I feel privileged to have been part of Arise Ministries' visit to Ireland. It was great fun, extremely humbling, at times sad, but more often than not, very happy and exciting. For me the one thing stands out is the day I saw a Catholic Priest in Ireland walk from his church carrying a well-beaten and well-read Bible in his hand. I was so excited and couldn't wait to hear this man speak because I knew he loved the Lord, and I was right!

Bless you Shirley for your encouragement and teaching but most of all your patience. You are a dear friend and will remain so always.

Psalm 133: *"How good and pleasant it is when brothers live together in unity."*

Gottfried Bernard, Solingen, Germany. Publisher

I was interpreting for Shirley at Africamp in Uganda 2005 when she shared how God had led her to seek reconciliation for her nation's past. We had a lot of technical difficulties at the time as the microphones kept going dead. I became very frustrated as I recognised this lady had something to offer the body of Christ and I desperately wanted to hear her story. As she spoke, the Holy Spirit seemed to fan the flames of revival in my heart and I so much wanted people in Germany to hear this. When she said she was writing a book, I quickly asked her if I could publish it in German. This is a story of simple obedience. Shirley did not wait until she was perfect to step out in faith, and I could see that what Shirley and her prayer partners have embarked upon is much bigger than they could handle themselves, so it must be of God. Her obedience and faith was a challenge to me personally, and it will also challenge the body of Christ in many nations. As God's people we need to walk out in obedience more and allow Him to enlarge what He has for each of us. This book has been as much of a struggle to publish as it was for Shirley to tell her story in Uganda, but we have never been discouraged. I pray that as you read it, your faith will grow and you will allow God to lead you on to bigger things.

Appendix

The following is a summary of the prophetic word that the Lord gave to John Mulinde concerning the Nations of Europe in 1996.

"One day as we prayed for Western Europe, I had a picture shown me in the spirit. I saw a map of the continent of Europe. As I looked there came out of the map a big pillar of smoke. It was a tall, thick, dark pillar of heavy black fumes as from a factory chimney. The fumes rose and spread out. From the pillar came a thin mist and it began spreading out almost imperceptibly, but within a short time it had formed a dark film over the entire continent of Europe. As the mist grew thicker the features below became blurred and difficult to distinguish.

Then suddenly I saw a small light spring out within the Isles of the UK. It grew rapidly with finger-like rays of light spreading out in all directions. The rays to the south spread out wider and with longer beams than the rest, and soon cut across the European mainland. For some time they disappeared into the thick cloud, and then they broke through and reappeared from within the fumes. They spread out even further touching across the entire African continent, eastwards across Asia and Australia and westwards across North and South America.

Then the picture disappeared as suddenly as it had appeared and in its place came the scripture Isaiah 60 v 1-5; *Arise, shine for your light has come, and the glory of the Lord rises upon you. See, darkness covers the earth and thick darkness is over the peoples. But the Lord rises upon you and His glory appears over you. Nations will come to your light and Kings to the brightness of your dawn. Lift up your eyes and look about you: All assemble and come to you, your sons come from afar, and your daughters are carried on the arm. Then you will look and be radiant, your heart will throb and swell with joy; the wealth on the seas will be brought to you, to you the riches of the nations will come.*

Later as John continued to seek God about the meaning of this picture, the Spirit of God spoke to him. He said that the picture was a representation of what was happening in the spiritual realm of Europe right now. The following is a summary of the revelation.

"A thick darkness is rising out of the continent of Europe right now. It is going to grow in intensity and will soon cover the whole continent, and the rest of the world. It is a force of evil. Wherever it will gain full control over the land, it will turn the hearts of the people totally away from God. However, the light that you saw is my power of renewal soon to be released upon the land and people of Europe. It will come if my people will give themselves whole-heartedly to seeking my face. Its' coming will be like a storm. It will be a mighty power against the darkness and will protect my people from the effect of the invasion of darkness. Wherever the light breaks out, the darkness shall be neutralised and defeated. This calls for the co-operation of my people in seeking for this to happen".

Later the Lord said to John. "Say to my people in Britain. *Arise and shine for the glory of the Lord is come upon you*", Isaiah 60 v 1-5.

"Yes" John says "I understood the Lord to be clearly calling Britain into a special place of responsibility. While the darkness is rising fast in the nations, many are losing all sense of direction. God will cause Britain to birth a new thing. A great light will spring out of Britain. It will be a wind of the Holy Spirit and will sweep across the whole of Europe like a bush fire. Indeed it shall stretch out to the ends of the world where it will join other fires in worldwide revival.

> If you will answer this call, oh Britain ...
> Give yourselves to institute prayer in your land ...
> And seek the Lord with all your heart ...
> With groaning and travailing prayer,

even as a woman in labour pains ...
Yes, if you will repent of your sins and iniquities ...
If you will heal the wounded hearts within you
And cause unity to abound among your people ...
Oh, if you will return to your redemptive purpose
And again be faithful to the work of being a witness of the Gospel in the nations ...

Then God will release upon you a mighty out-pouring of His Spirit.

You will again be clothed with the Glory of the Lord.

You will be a nation that bears the name of the Lord like a banner in the sky.

Other nations will see what God is doing in you. Yes, those that are struggling against the domineering darkness looming over their territories will call to you for help and assistance. Then you will be used by the Lord to bring light and redemption to many, even as in the olden days. That is God's redemptive purpose for you.

There are many in Europe and beyond who would choose Christ given a fair chance, but they are still blinded and cannot see Christ. There are many too, who are Christians but are weak, wounded and weary, they have no strength to resist.

If you will rise up to the challenge then the Lord will use you to take Light to such as these. Then even if the rising darkness covers their land, they will survive its destructive influence because of the revival power of God. Such is the responsibility God is laying upon you; to birth the revival that will spread out to the rest of Europe.

If you do not rise up to your calling God will let you go, as He said in Proverbs 1: 22-33. God will cause Judgement to come upon you, Britain, for having neglected and forsaken your destiny as a great Missionary Nation, and for not paying heed when God offered you an opportunity of Grace.

It was God's plan from the beginning to use you to take the Good News to the nations of the world. That is why from the beginning He allowed you great authority as a maritime nation;

that you may travel far and wide. It was his hand that allowed you to establish an empire covering almost the entire world. It was not just for your pride, but so that in the process, you may win over the peoples of those nations to Him. Yes, it was even Him that blessed your language ENGLISH into becoming the most widely spoken language in the world. He intended to use it as a medium of communication, effectively linking the peoples of the world. Your great missionaries were used to Christianise many lands. Your Statesmen helped to end the slave trade, and to lay a foundation from which the people of God within the nations are rising to make their contribution to world evangelisation. There is a lot for you to repent of in what you did in the nations but the good things remain, nevertheless.

Look what Britain has become today. Once a great Christian nation, you have permitted many things to slip away. Very often you turned a deaf ear against all warnings to safeguard what is good and still remains of your great Christian heritage. You have already lost a great deal of that heritage, and a lot more will certainly go if you do not take quick action to redeem it. If you will not repent, Britain, you will certainly not escape God's judgement, and will be a victim of the very powers you were called to defeat.

Look your sons and daughters come from afar and gather themselves unto you. These I understand to be people from the lands once ruled by the UK stretching across the Americas, Africa, Asia and Australia. They will again form a holy alliance with you and in this networking great and mighty things shall some to pass.

Many will come from Africa and the rest of the "Third World" and will be used by the Lord God to bless you spiritually. In some places they will take over your abandoned places of worship and will bring new life to them and great blessing in revival. That is why the Lord says (Is. 60 verse 5) *"then you shall see, and flow together, and your heart shall fear, and be enlarged"*

This will demand great humbling on your part, but your God shall lift you up. These are the last days and God is calling every nation to take up its position in God's redemptive purpose and fulfil their calling. You are not the first nation in God's calling, but neither are you the last. Do not let pride hinder you. Look at the gifting God has allowed you to acquire over the years, and the unique position you hold in relation to Europe, America and indeed Asia. Turn now and do not allow yourself to miss God's timing. All Europe is going to pass through a very painful struggle between two aggressive forces - light v darkness. God has called you to play a crucial role, so arise!

About Arise Ministries

Arise Ministries is a small group of Christians of mixed denominations dedicated to prayer, healing and reconciliation. We are based in Huntingdon, England, the birthplace of the 17th Century leader Oliver Cromwell. Shirley Bowers is the leader, and Rev Scott Watts is the pastor. We have many prayer partners around the globe.

Cromwell was a devout Puritan who boasted he fought his battles in the name of Christ, led by the Holy Ghost (Spirit). He is, and will always be, a controversial figure. We are not pro- or anti-Cromwell, but over the years we have discovered that this part of our history has left consequences that affect people today. We believe that we have been called by God to address this and go to places such as Ireland and elsewhere in order to bring healing and reconciliation. God has shown us that where His name was used to bring death and destruction, we through repentance and love can sow life and hope.

We do not have any magic formula; we are just ordinary people with an extraordinary God who seek to be obedient to His call. The scripture 2 Chronicles 7:14 (*"If my people, who are called by my name, will humble themselves and pray and seek my face, and turn from their wicked ways, then will I hear from Heaven, forgive their sin and heal their land."*) sums up our mission and our vision.

The name "Arise Ministries" comes from the scripture given to our nation Isaiah 60:1 *"ARISE, shine, for your light has come, and the glory of the Lord rises upon you."* We long to see unity spread throughout the body of Christ, so that as barriers come down, we can arise as God's people and be the church God has called us to be.

For further information go to www.ariseministries.co.uk

1997 Uganda

President hands flag
over to conference
as sign of handing
nation to God

2002 Huntingdon

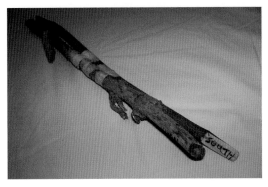

Sticks representing
North and South of
Ireland are propheti-
cally bound together

2002 Ireland

Shirley and Arise team
with Mayor Malachy
Godfrey and
Fr Paddy Kiery

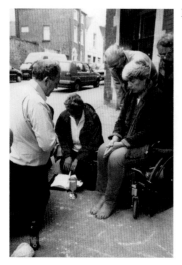

Edward washes Katie's feet

A bouquet of roses for Shirley

Door of Reconciliation in
St Patrick's cathedral

Attendees of service at
Franciscan Friary

Wexford contacts and Arise team members.
L to R; Katie, Pat Murphy, Shirley, Annette, Vanessa, Phyllis, Georgina and
Stephen Forbes, and Beryl (back of her head)

Team with Patricia
Finnerty
(L to R; Phyllis, Lance,
Beryl, Annette, Shir-
ley, Patricia, Katie)

Team welcomed to Cork

Giving key to Sister Bridget

Shirley with Philip Lynch as she presented letter to councillors Tommy Maher and Jimmy Brett

Phyllis, Shirley and
Fr Dan Carroll

Shirley gives Mayor of
Kilkenny, Betty Man-
ning, a key

(This photo is printed courtesy of
The Kilkenny People)

Shirley presents key of
unity to Fr Richard
Scriven, Rev Norman
Lynas and Methodist
minister Rev Stephen
Taylor

Act of reconciliation
on bridge at Athlone

Flag reads
"It is finished"
at Darkley House
near Crossmaglen

2003 Huntingdon

Rev Robin Mann,
Stephen and
Georgina Forbes

Cllr Frank Godfrey and Malachy Godfrey, Mayor of Drogheda, offer hand of friendship to Jeff Dutton, Mayor of Huntingdon

2003 Ireland

Frank Godfrey and Tom Reilly shake hands, with Shirley, Mayoress of Huntingdon Claire Dutton and Mayor of Drogheda Maria Campbell-O'Brien

Arise Team with Fr Danny McDonald and the Mayler chalice

2005 Uganda

Our family in
Kampala

Gottfried and Shirley

Joseph makes a covenant to pray for
England (with Shirley and Annette)

Praying with Jovelet